GUITAR THEORY 1

2nd Edition | SANDY FELDSTEIN AARON STANG

The Most Complete Guitar Course Available

- Correlates with *21st Century Guitar Method 1*
- Helps beginners understand music theory in a practical way
- Relates music notation and diagrams to the actual guitar fretboard
- Workbook-style format
- 2nd edition updated with new lesson material

Contents

Belwin™
a division of Alfred

Alfred Music
P.O. Box 10003
Van Nuys, CA 91410-0003
alfred.com

ISBN-10: 1-4706-3366-3 (Book)
ISBN-13: 978-1-4706-3366-0 (Book)

Cover photo: Robert Santos

Use after page 6 of
Belwin's 21st Century Guitar Method 1.

Music Notation

Music is written on a five-line staff. Between each line is a space.

Number the lines and spaces below:

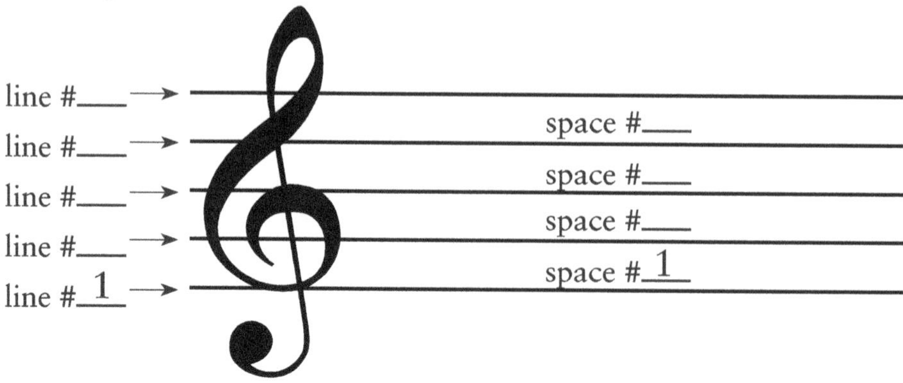

At the beginning of each staff is a clef. The treble clef encircles the second line, which is the note G, as you see below. Therefore, the treble clef is sometimes called the G clef.

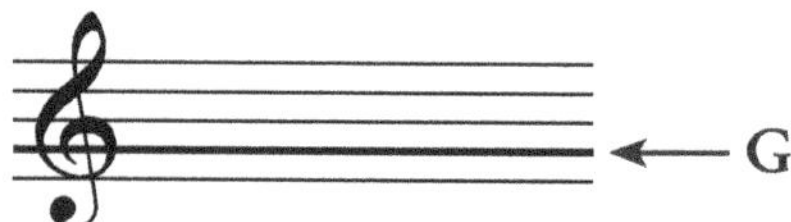

Notes are named after the first seven letters of the alphabet (A through G):

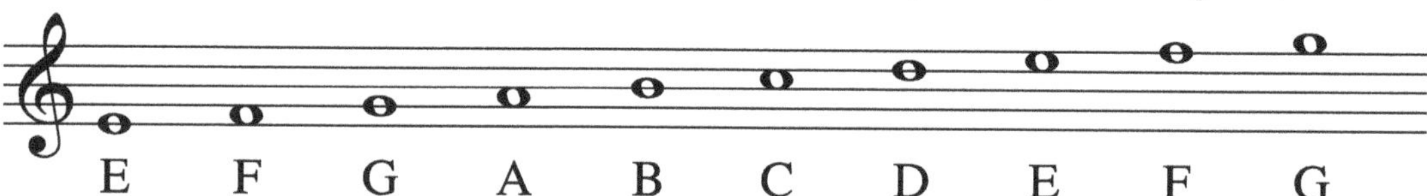

Draw the notes of the musical alphabet:

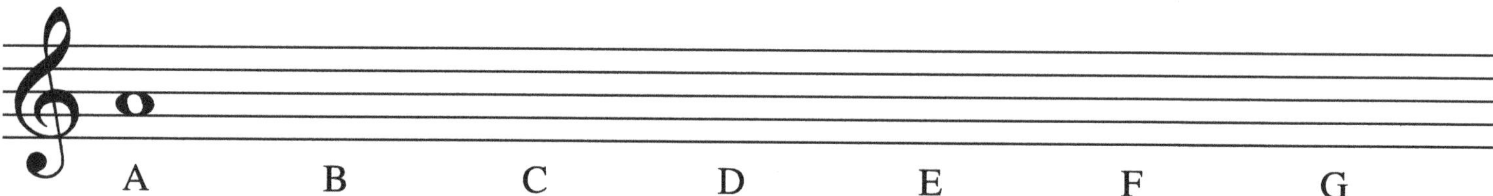

Music is divided into equal parts called *measures*.
Bar lines indicate the beginning and end of measures.

The space between two bar lines is called a measure.
Double bar lines, with one thin and one thick line, mark the end of a piece.

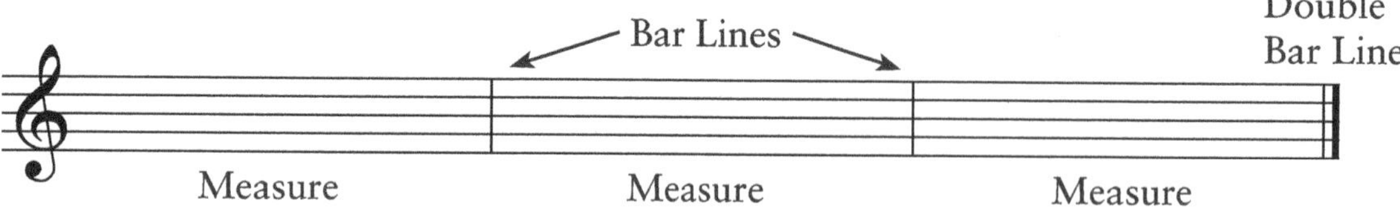

1. Divide the staff below into seven measures.
2. Name the notes.
3. End the staff with a double bar line.

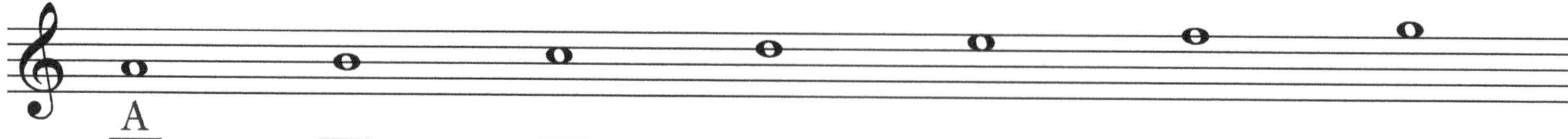

Use after page 7 of
Belwin's 21st Century Guitar Method 1.

Rhythm Notation and Time Signatures

At the beginning of every song is a *time signature*. ¼ is the most common time signature:

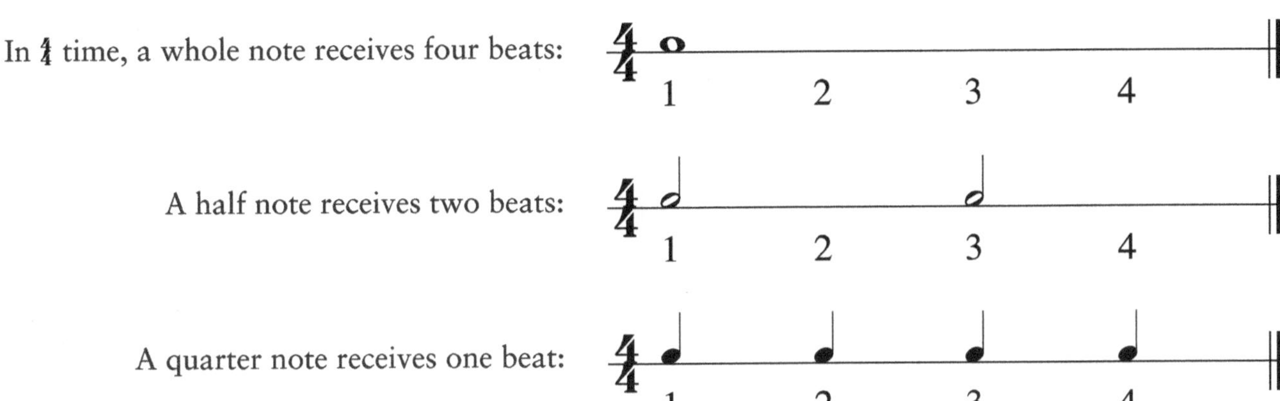

In ¼ time, a whole note receives four beats:

A half note receives two beats:

A quarter note receives one beat:

In the following three exercises, fill in the beats under the notes. Remember, there are four beats in each measure.

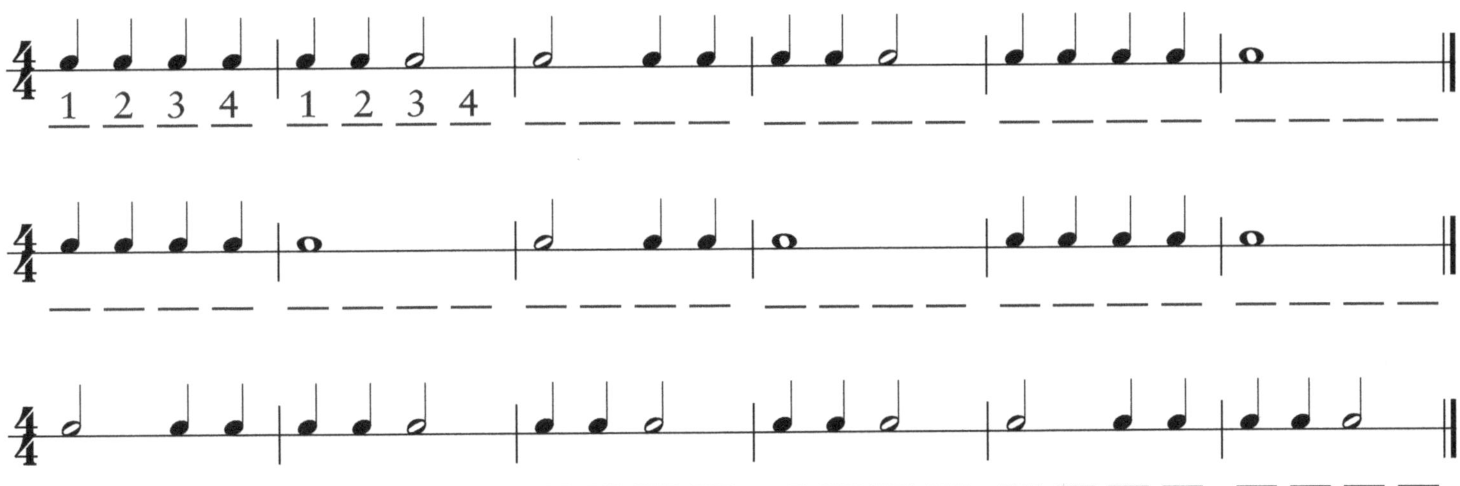

Add bar lines in the appropriate places (every four beats). End with a double bar.

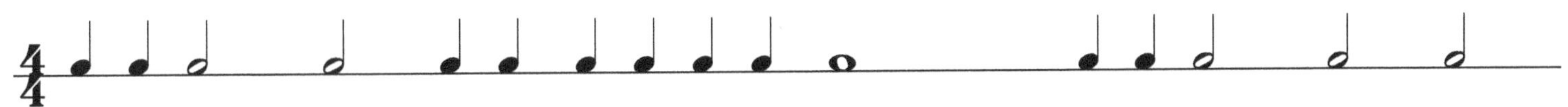

Add bar lines (every four beats), then name the notes.

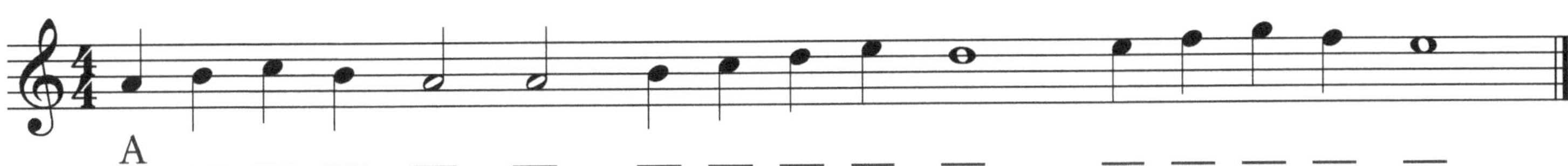

The Notes on the 1st String

Use after page 8 of
Belwin's 21st Century Guitar Method 1.

Name the notes indicated on the treble staff:

 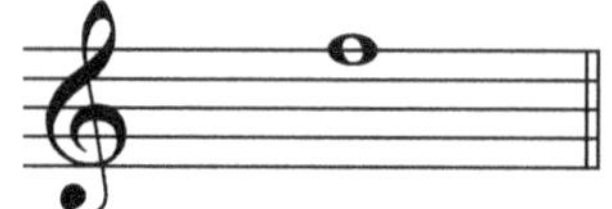 

This fretboard diagram indicates a note played with the ___ finger at the ___ fret of the ___ string. Its note name is ___ . Play the note and say its name.

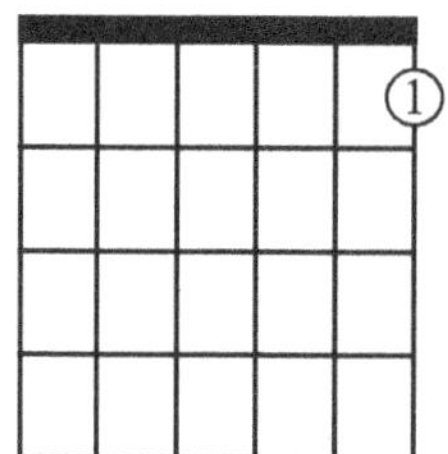

HOW TO READ FRETBOARD DIAGRAMS

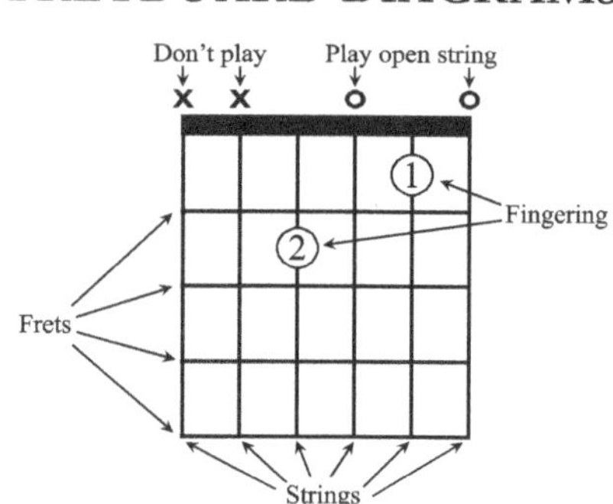

This tablature indication shows that the ___ string is to be played at the ___ fret. It will sound the note ___ . Play the note and say its name.

Name the notes indicated in the fretboard diagrams to the right:

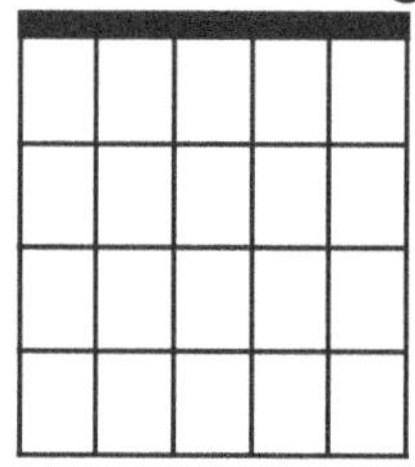 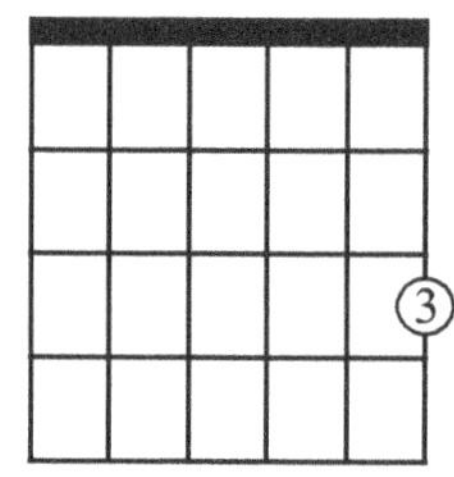

Draw the notes indicated in the tablature on the treble staves:

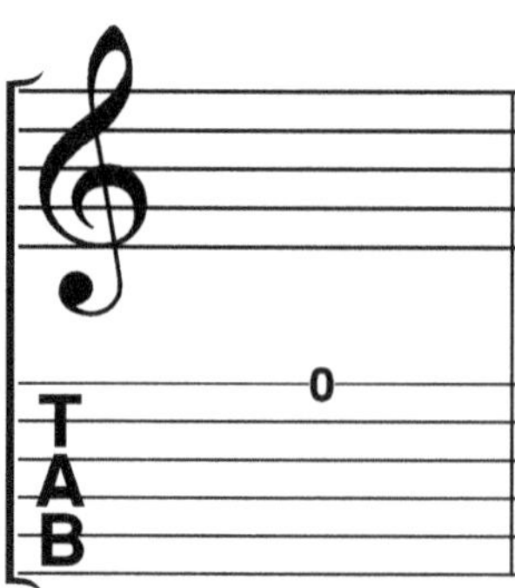  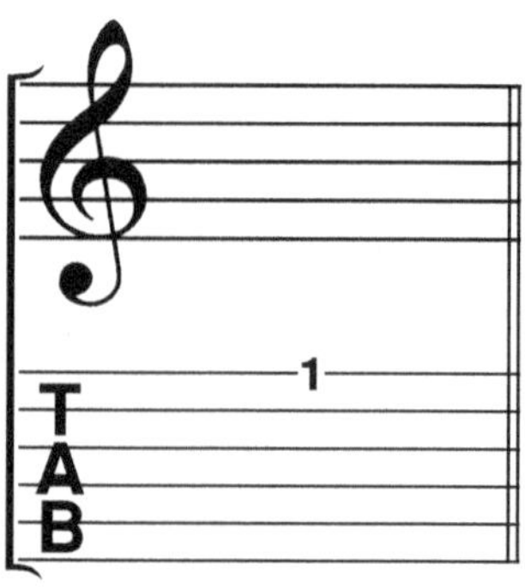

Name the notes and play them.

The Notes on the 2nd String

Name the indicated notes:

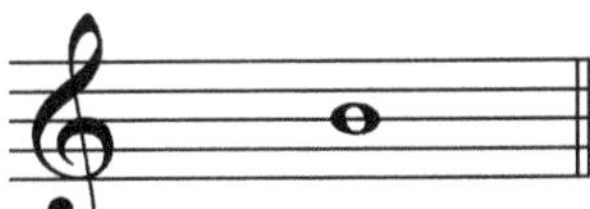  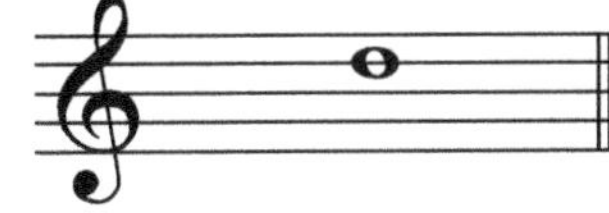

___   ___   ___

This fretboard diagram indicates a note played with the ___ finger at the ___ fret of the ___ string. Its note name is ___ . Play the note and say its name.

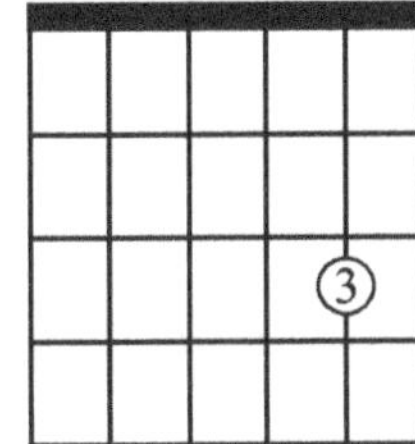

This tablature indication shows that the ___ string is to be played at the ___ fret. It will sound the note ___ . Play the note and say its name.

Name the notes indicated in the fretboard diagrams to the right:

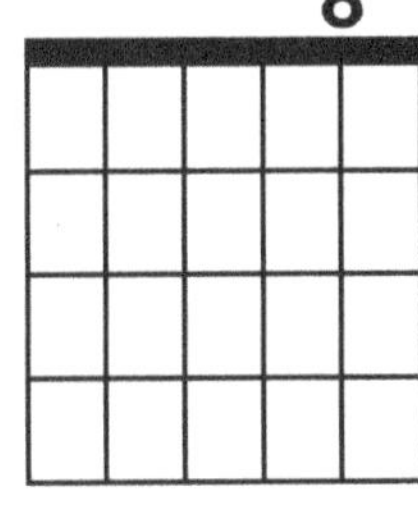 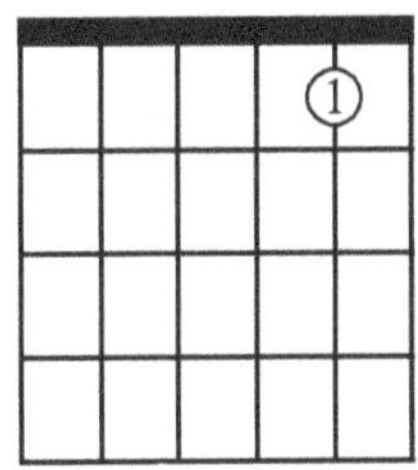

___   ___

Notate the indicated notes in the tablature:

___   ___   ___

Name the notes and play them.

Use after pages 12 and 13 of
Belwin's 21st Century Guitar Method 1.

Tied Notes

A *tie* is a curved line that connects two adjacent notes of the same pitch. Hold the two notes as though they are one.

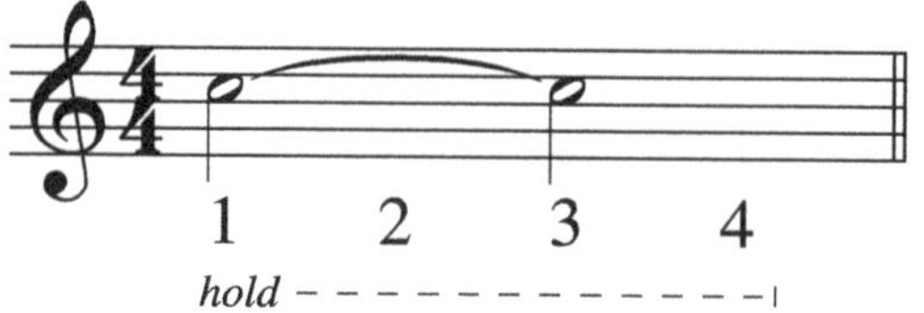

Add the beats of the tied notes:

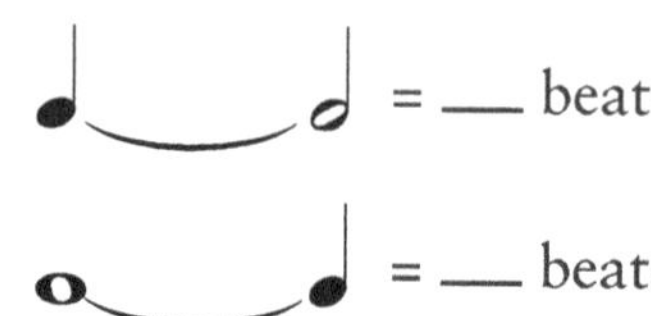

= __3__ beats

= ___ beats

= ___ beats

= ___ beats

Draw the note that equals the number of beats of the tied notes:

Pickup Notes

The opening measures of "When the Saints Go Marching In" contain pickup notes and ties.
    1. Draw the bar lines.
    2. Write the counting above the staff.
    3. Name the notes below the staff.

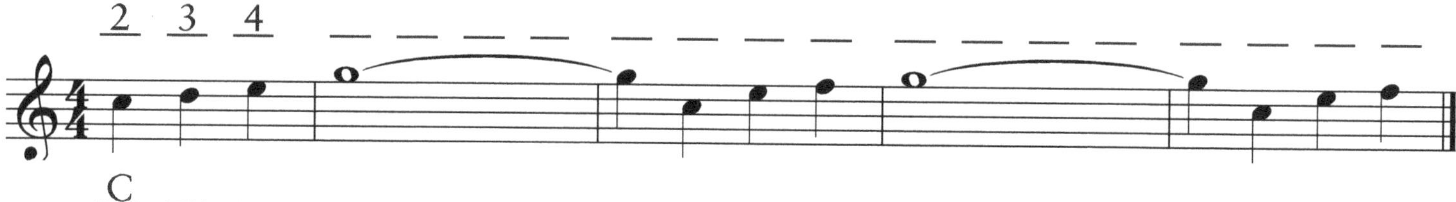

Note Review

1. Draw the note indicated on the fretboard diagram.
2. Place the correct fret number on the correct string in the tablature.
3. Name the note and play it.

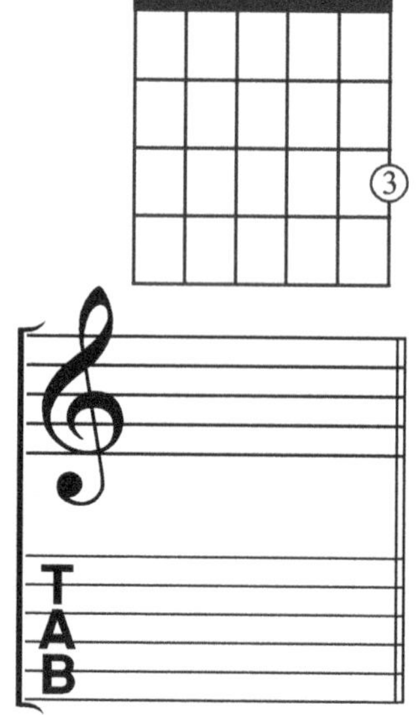

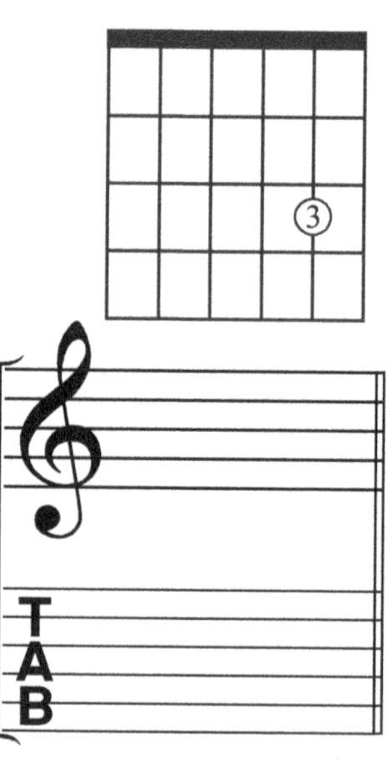

Use after page 14 of
Belwin's 21st Century Guitar Method 1.

The Notes on the 3rd String

Draw the indicated notes:

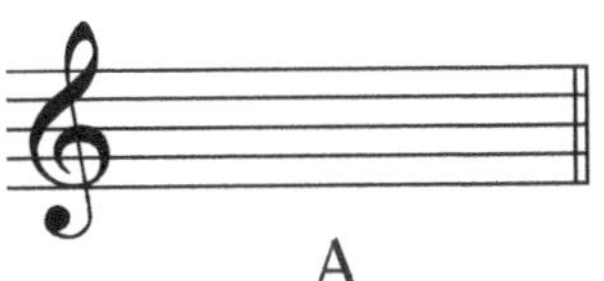

<u>A</u>

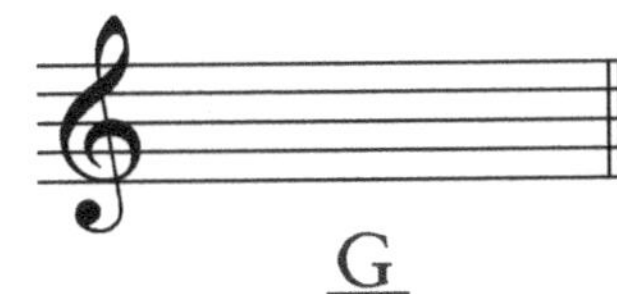

<u>G</u>

This fretboard diagram indicates a note played with the ___ finger at the ___ fret of the ___ string. Its note name is ___ . Play the note and say its name.

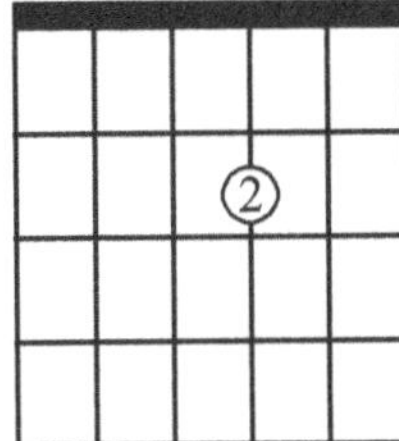

This tablature indication shows that the ___ string is to be played *open*. It will sound the note ___ . Play the note and say its name.

The note indicated in the guitar frame is: ___ .

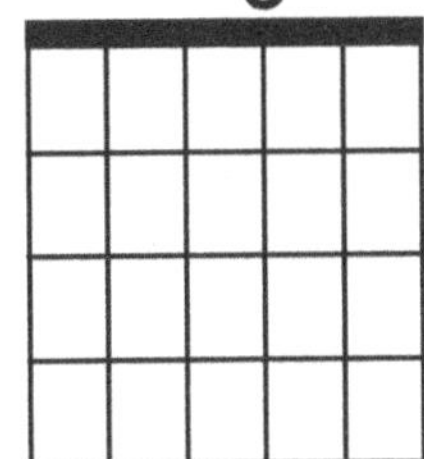

Draw G on the treble staff:

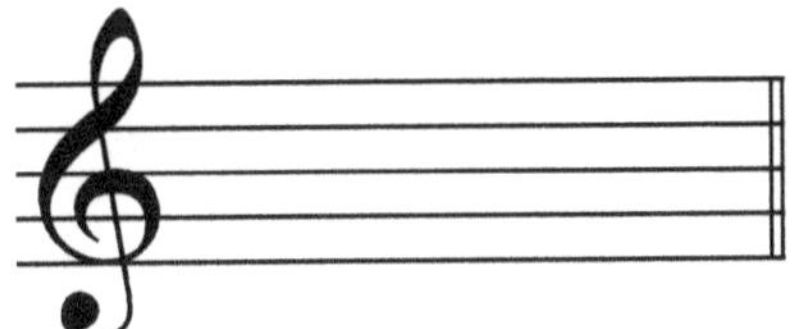

Note Review

For every note indicated in the tablature:
1. Indicate the correct finger at the correct fret on the fretboard diagram.
2. Draw the note on the treble staff.
3. Name the note and play it.

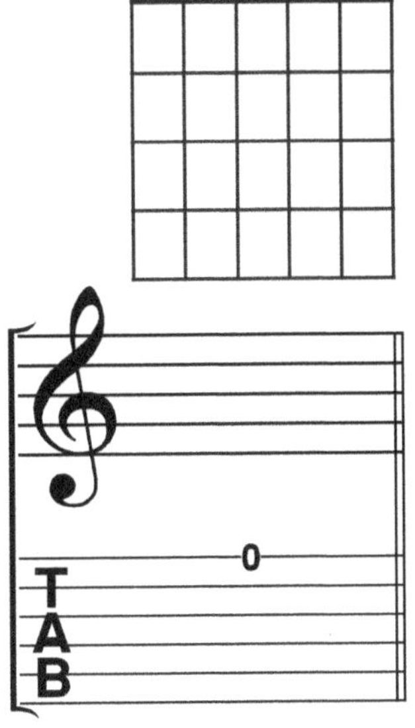

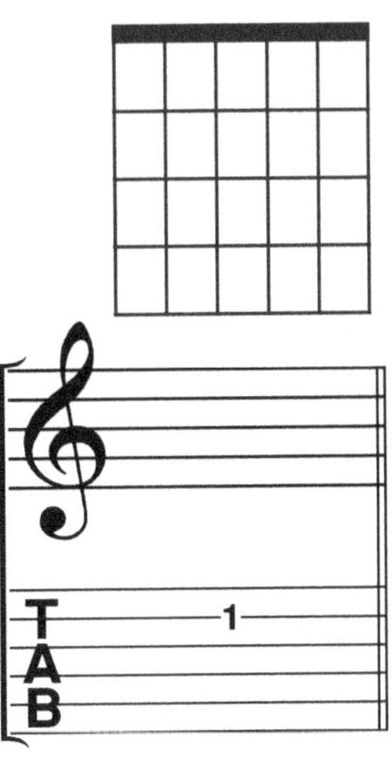

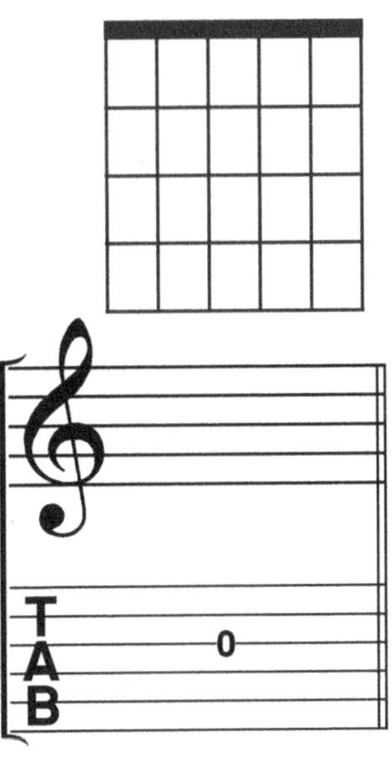

Use after page 16 of
Belwin's 21st Century Guitar Method 1.

The Dotted Half Note

A *dot* placed after a note adds one half the value of the original note. A dotted half note (♩.) equals three counts.

Write the beats under the notes:

New Time Signature: ¾

THREE COUNTS TO A MEASURE

A QUARTER NOTE RECEIVES ONE COUNT

In ¾ time, a half note receives two beats:

A quarter note receives one beat:

Write the beats under the notes below. Remember, there are three beats in each measure.

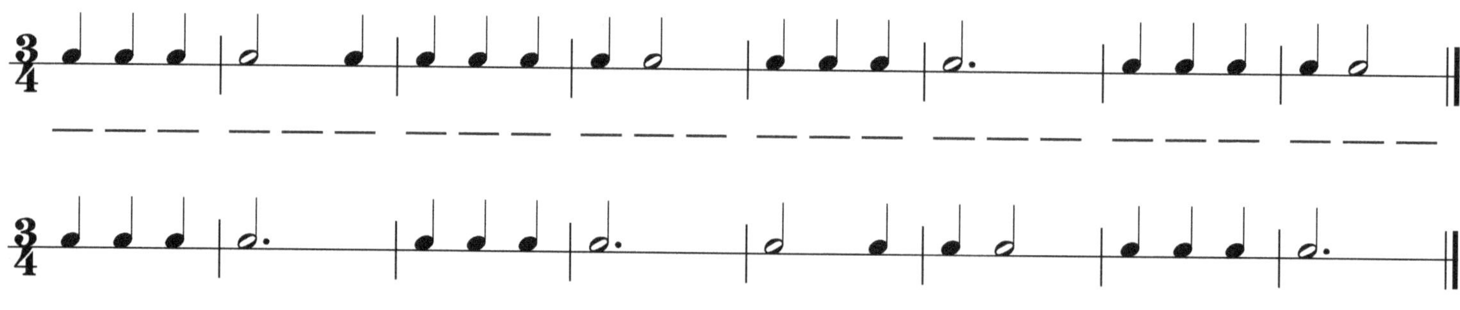

Add bar lines and name the notes in the following two musical excerpts.
End each line with a double bar.

Play the excerpts.

Use after page 18 of
Belwin's 21st Century Guitar Method 1.

Repeat Signs

Two dots placed before a double bar line 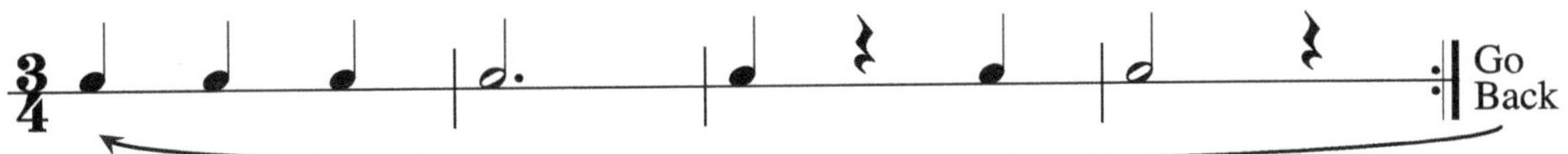
means go back to the beginning and play again.
These are called *repeat signs*.

This is an excerpt from a well-known song:

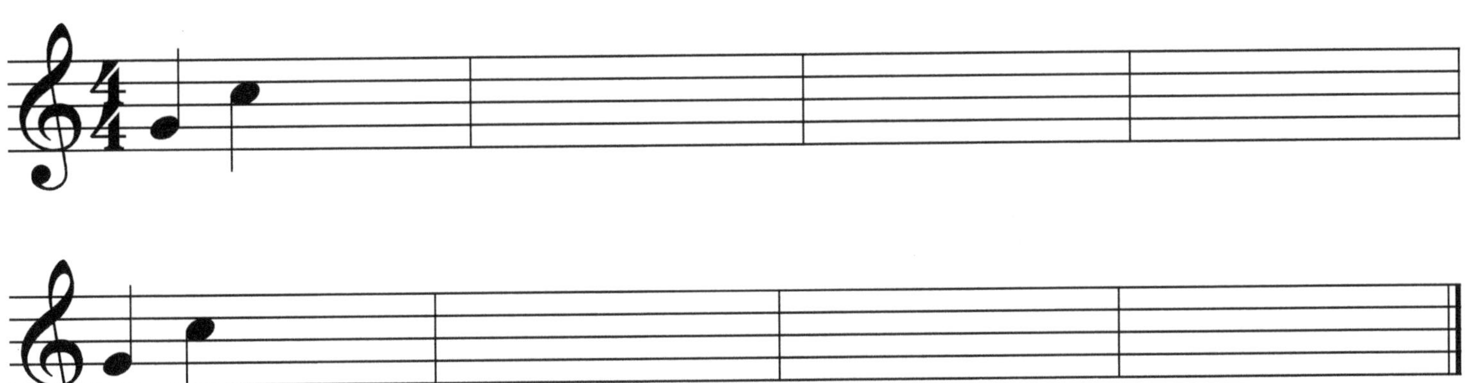

Below, write the excerpt as it would appear *without* using a repeat sign.
(Some notes are indicated as a guide.)

Play the song. Can you name it?

New Note: A

Indicate the note A
in the tablature:

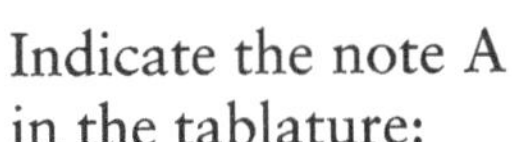

Indicate the note A
on the diagram:

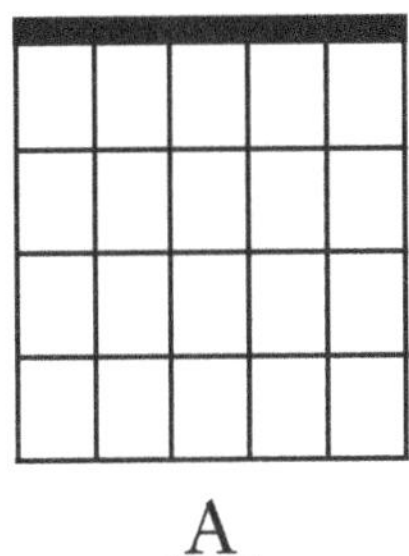

The Notes on the 4th String:

Use after page 20 of
Belwin's 21st Century Guitar Method 1.

Name the notes indicated on the treble staff:

  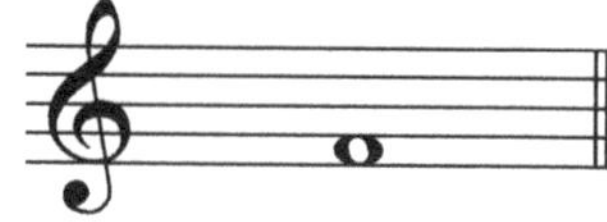

This fretboard diagram indicates a note played with the ___ finger at the ___ fret of the ___ string. Its note name is ___ . Play the note and say its name.

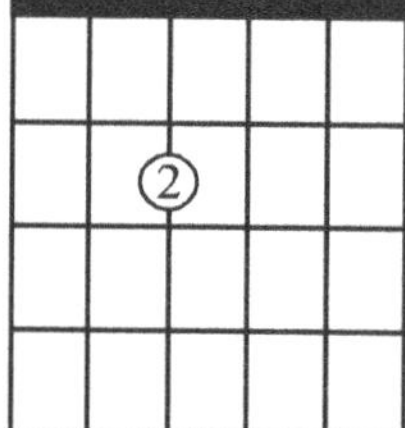

This tablature indication shows that the ___ string is to be played at the ___ fret. It will sound the note ___ . Play the note and say its name.

Name the notes indicated in the fretboard diagrams to the right:

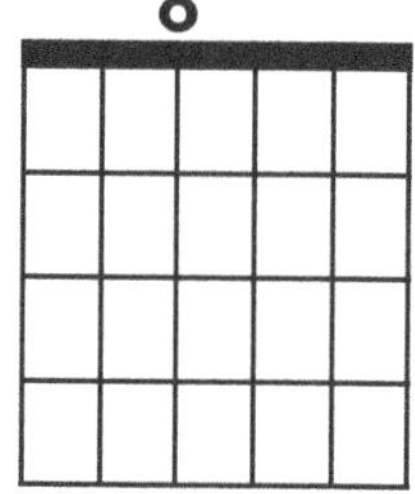 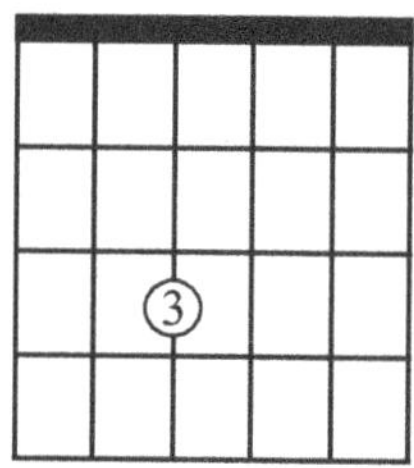

Draw the notes indicated in the tablature on the treble staves:

Name the notes and play them.

Use after page 22 of
Belwin's 21st Century Guitar Method 1.

Eighth Notes

One eighth note looks like a quarter note with a flag added to its stem:

Groups of two or four eighth notes are joined by a beam:

Two eighth notes equal one quarter note:

Four eighth notes equal one half note:

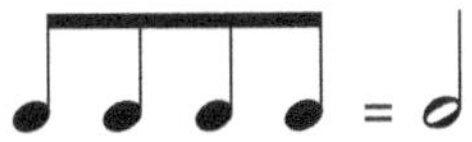

Eight eighth notes equal one whole note:

In ¾ time, an eighth note receives half a beat:

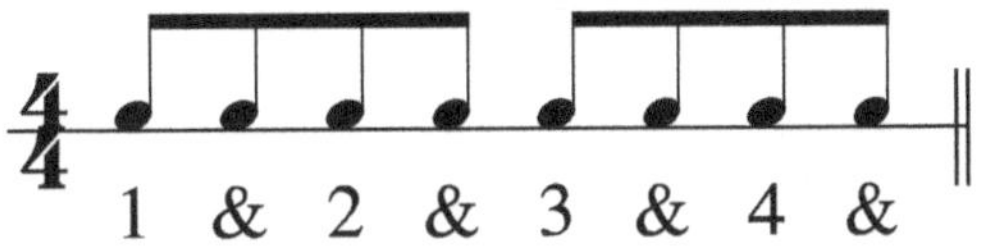

1 & 2 & 3 & 4 &

Write the beats under the notes:

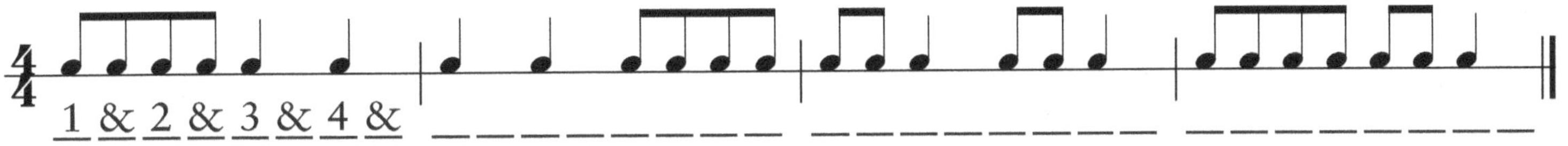

1 & 2 & 3 & 4 &

Below, add the bar lines in the appropriate places. End with a double bar.

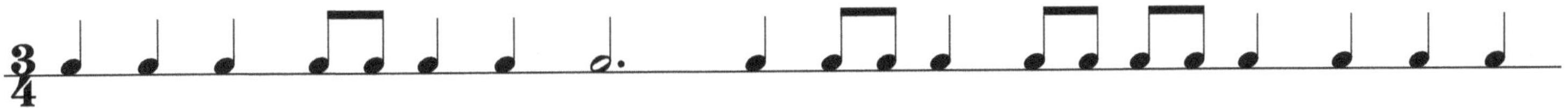

Add the beats:

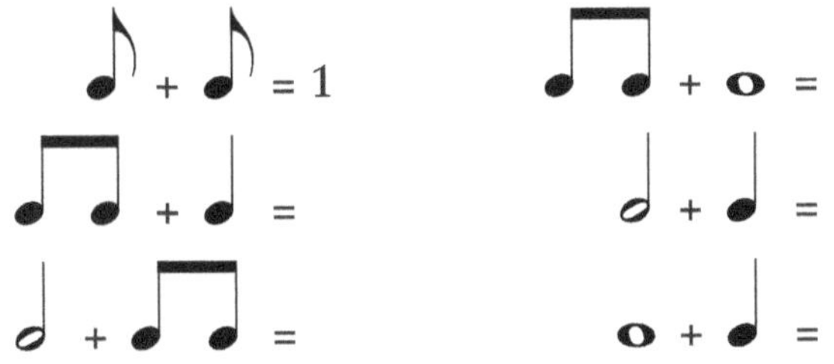

♪ + ♪ = 1

+ o =

+ =

+ =

+ =

+ =

Draw the note value that equals the number of beats:

♪ + ♪ =

+ =

+ =

+ =

Add bar lines and name the notes in the following musical excerpt:

Play the excerpt.

Use after page 23 of
Belwin's 21st Century Guitar Method 1.

More Repeat Signs

Sometimes, you repeat back to another repeat sign.

Below is a melody that uses multiple repeat signs.

On the blank staff below, write the above piece of music as it would appear without
using the repeat signs. (Some notes are indicated as a guide.)

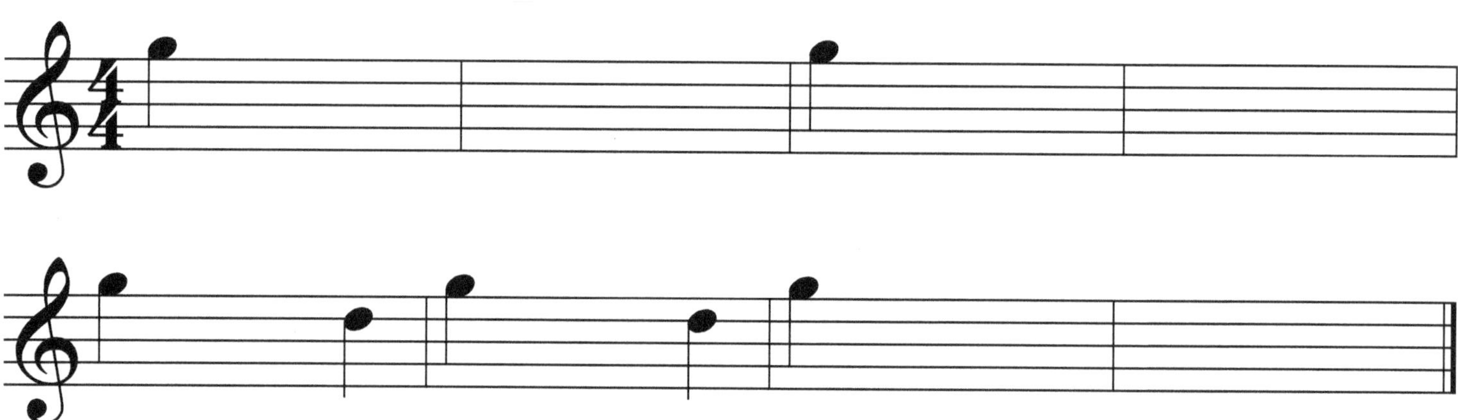

Review

1. Draw the note on each treble staff below.
2. Place the fret number on the correct string in the tablature.
3. Name the note and play it.

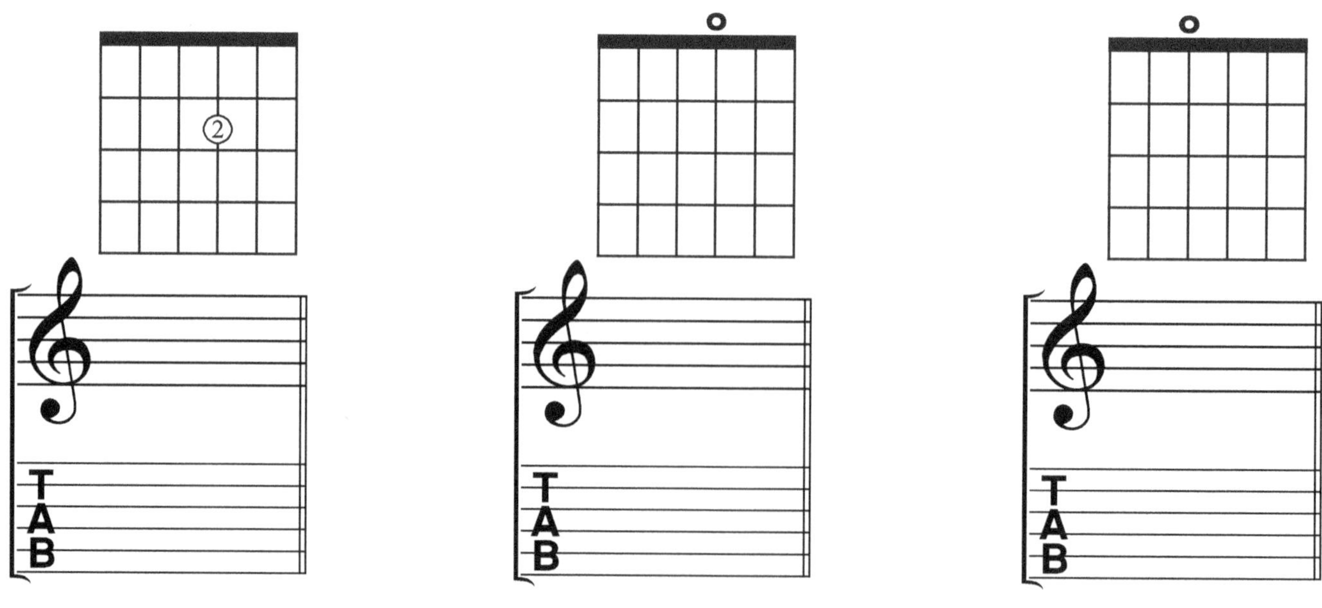

Sharp Sign

A *sharp sign* (♯) raises the pitch of a note a half step.

When saying a sharp note's name, we say the letter name first and the sharp next—for instance, F-sharp. When we write it in music notation, the sharp sign comes first.

To draw a sharp, draw two vertical lines:	Then add the slanted lines:	Draw sharps before both F's:

Name the indicated notes:

__ __ __ __ __ __ __

Draw the indicated notes:

Key Signature

When the F♯ is indicated at the beginning of a piece of music, it means every F note in the piece is played F♯.

The key of G contains one sharp: 

Write the key signature for the key of G:

Name the notes below:

__ __ __ __ __ __ __   __ __ __ __ __ __ __   __ __

Rhythm Review

Fill in the missing beats in the example below with the appropriate notes. Each measure should contain four counts.

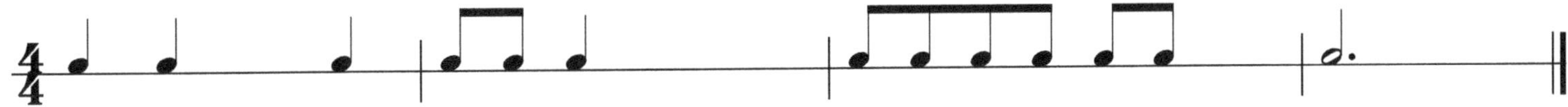

Fill in the missing beats in the example below with the appropriate notes. Each measure should contain three counts.

Use after pages 23 and 25 of *Belwin's 21st Century Guitar Method 1.*

Use after page 26 of
Belwin's 21st Century Guitar Method 1.

The C, G, and G7 Chords

The C, G, and G7 chords are illustrated on the fretboard diagrams below. Draw the indicated notes on the music staff:

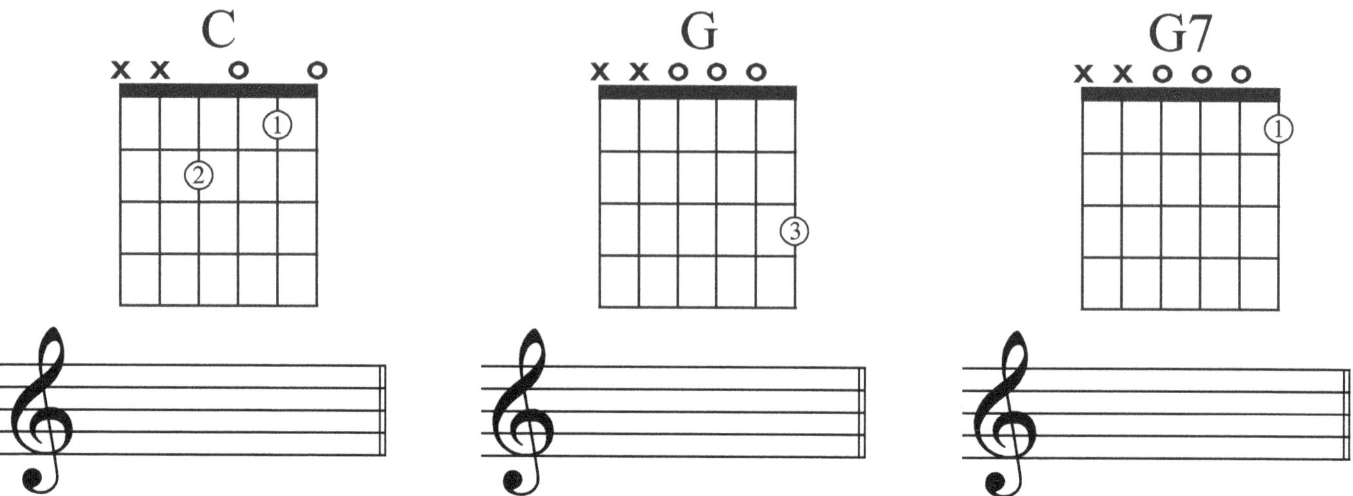

1. Notate, on the tablature, the chords indicated in the treble staff.
2. Name the chords.

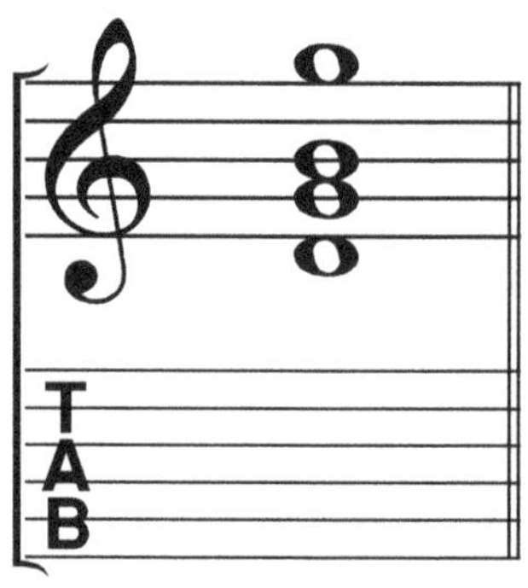

Fill in the fretboard diagrams, which are called *chord frame diagrams* when used for chords, to illustrate how the chords are fingered on the guitar fretboard:

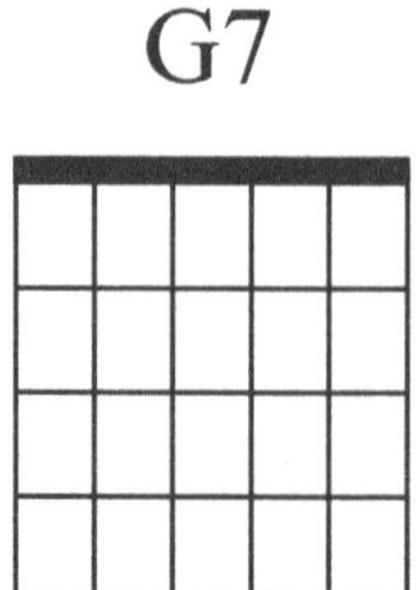

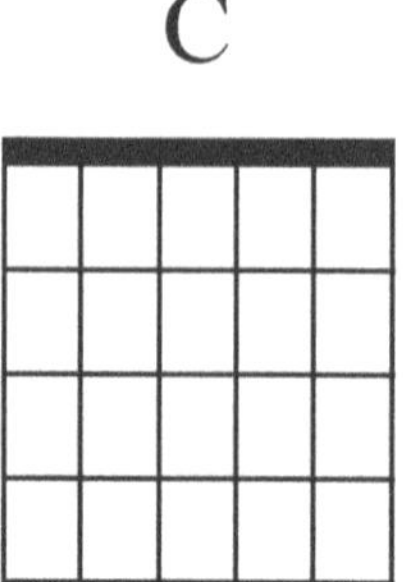

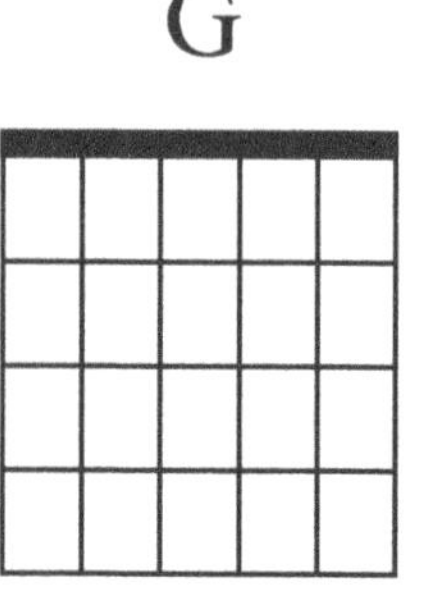

Use after page 27 of
Belwin's 21st Century Guitar Method 1.

The D and D7 Chords

1. Notate, on the tablature, the chords indicated in the treble staff.
2. Name the chords.

___   ___

Fill in the chord frame diagrams to illustrate how the chords are fingered on the guitar fretboard:

D

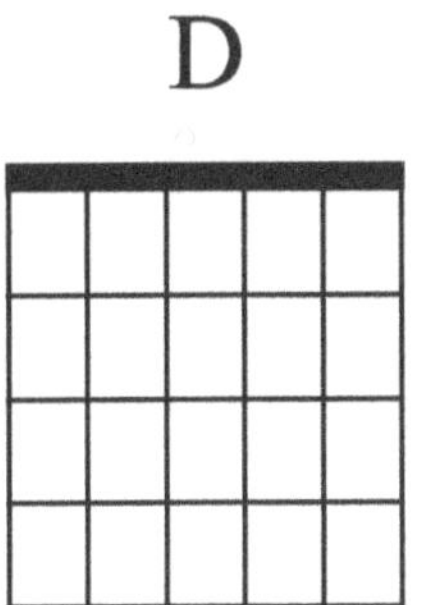

D7

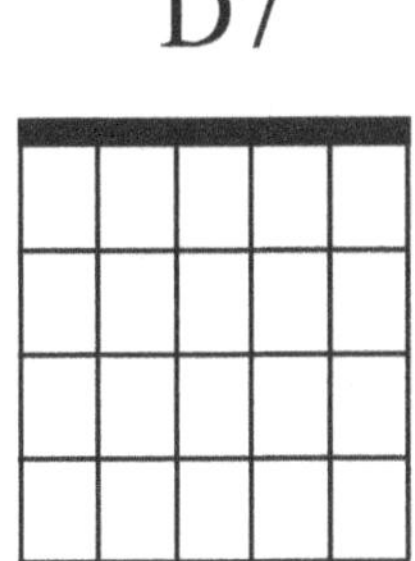

The D and D7 chords are illustrated on the chord frame diagrams below. Fill in the notes on the music staff:

D

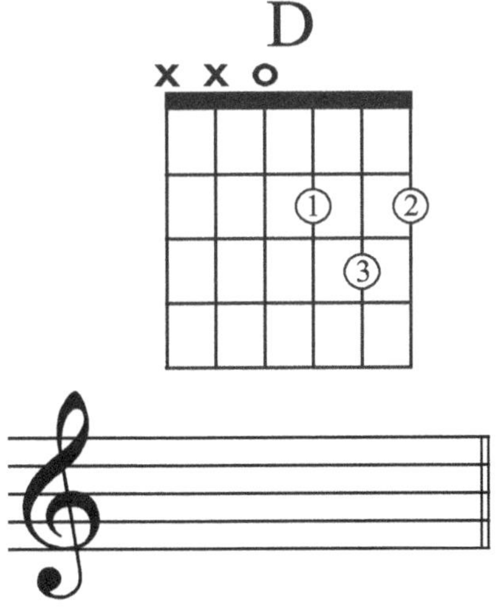

D7

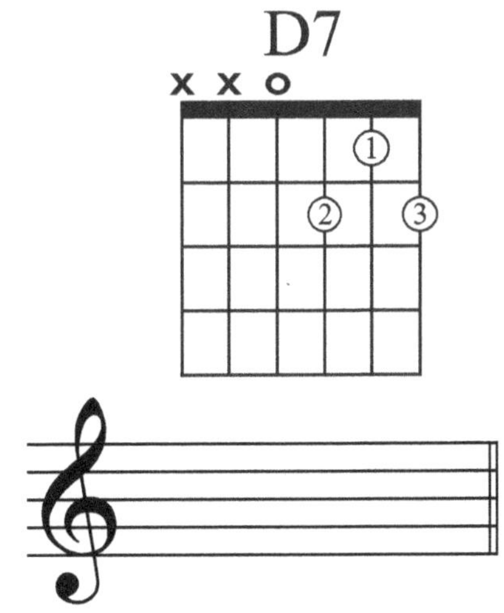

Use after page 29 of
Belwin's 21st Century Guitar Method 1.

The E Chord Shape and Flamenco Chords

Fill in the chord frame diagrams below to illustrate how the indicated chords are fingered on the guitar fretboard. Then, follow the rhythm slashes to play "One-Shape Spanish Fantasy."

One-Shape Spanish Fantasy

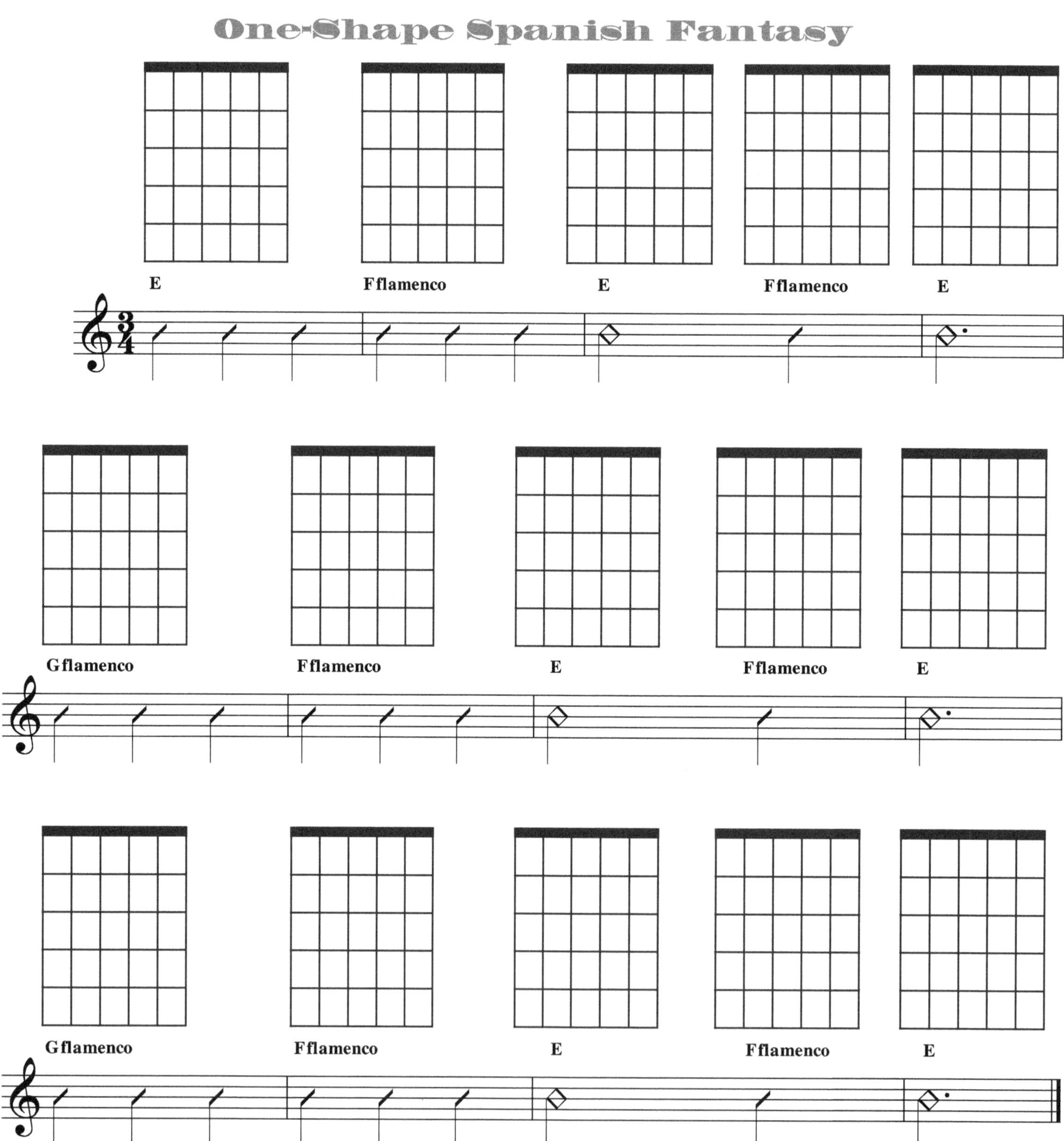

The Notes on the 5th String

Name the indicated notes:

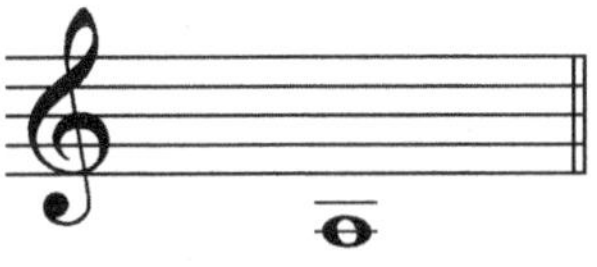

____   ____   ____

This fretboard diagram indicates a note played with the ___ finger at the ___ fret of the ___ string. Its note name is ___ . Play the note and say its name.

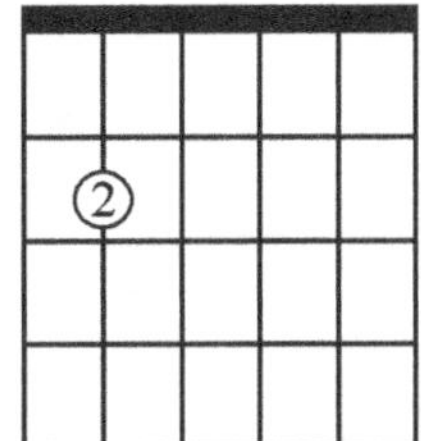

This tablature indication shows that the ___ string is to be played at the ___ fret. It will sound the note ___ . Play the note and say its name.

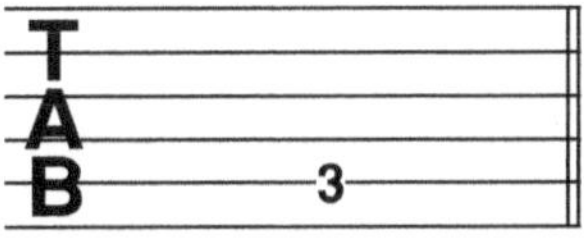

Name the notes indicated in the fretboard diagrams to the right:

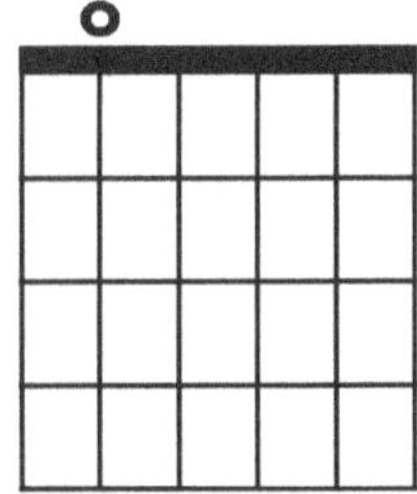
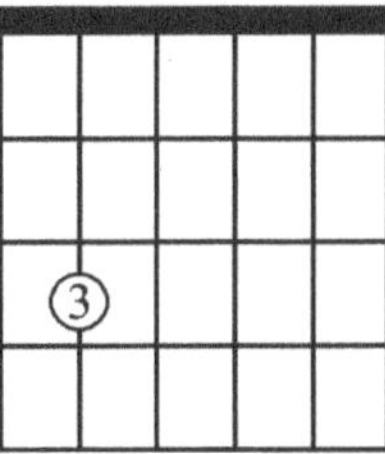

____   ____

Draw the notes indicated in the tablature on the treble staves:

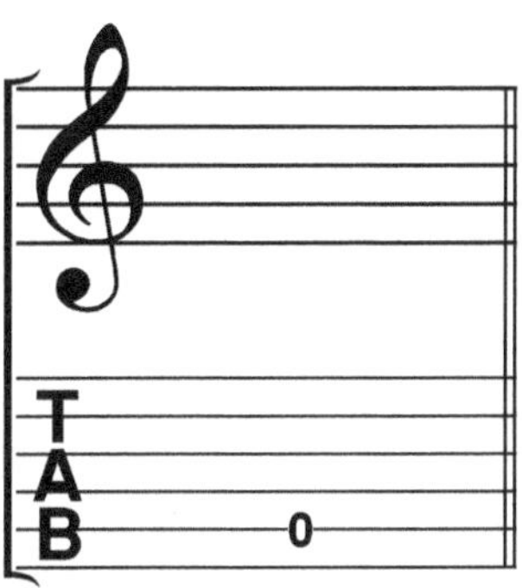

____   ____   ____

Name the notes and play them.

The C, A Minor, and D Minor Chords

Use after page 32 of
Belwin's 21st Century Guitar Method 1.

The C (now in the full five-string form), A Minor (Am), and D Minor (Dm) chords are illustrated in the chord frame diagrams below. Draw the indicated notes on the music staff:

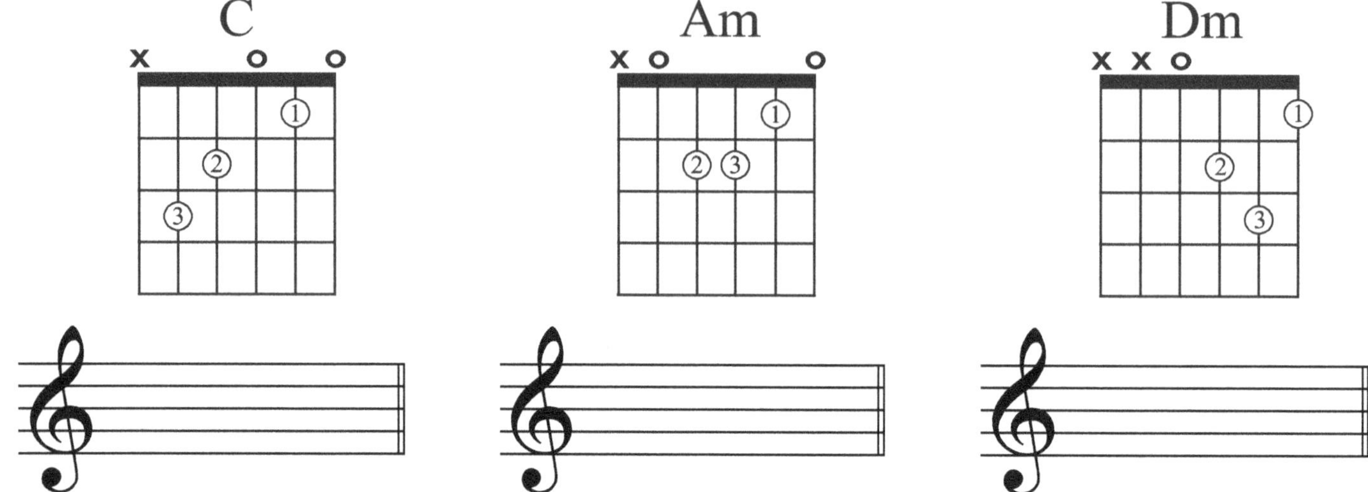

1. Notate, on the tablature, the chords indicated in the treble staff.
2. Name the chords.

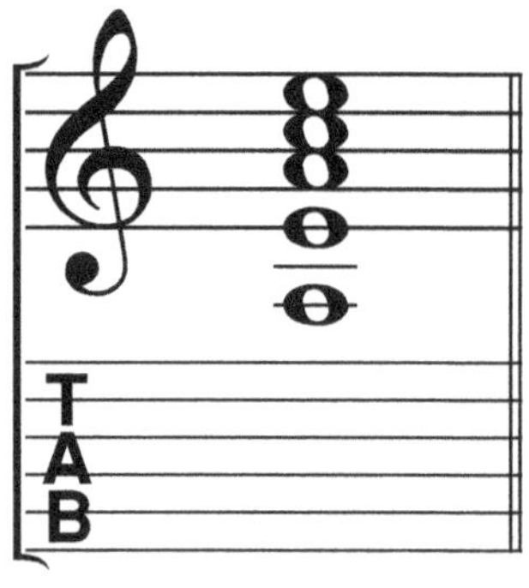
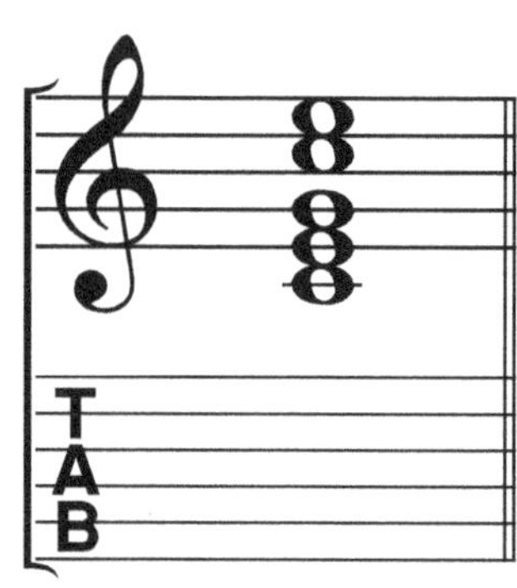
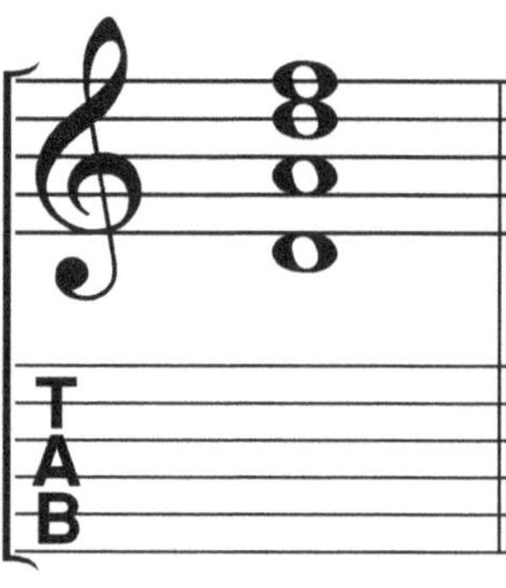

Fill in the chord frame diagrams to illustrate how the chords are fingered on the guitar fretboard:

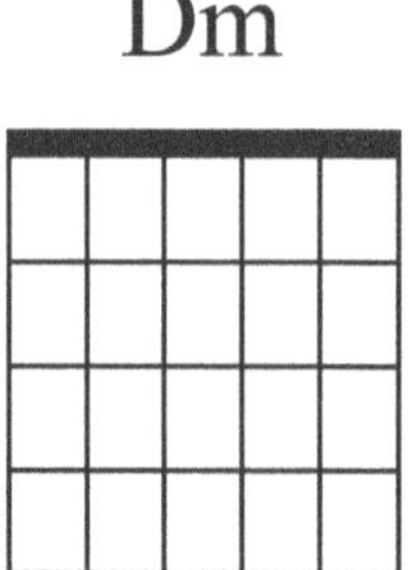

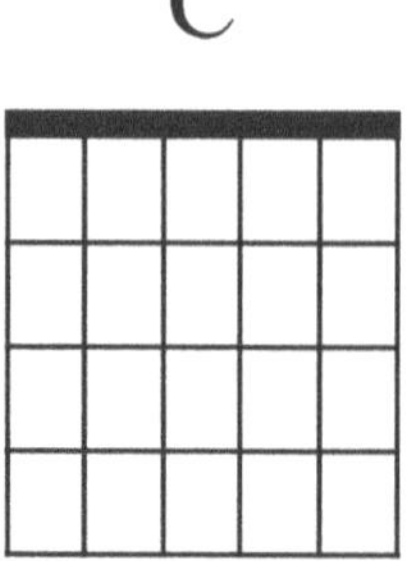

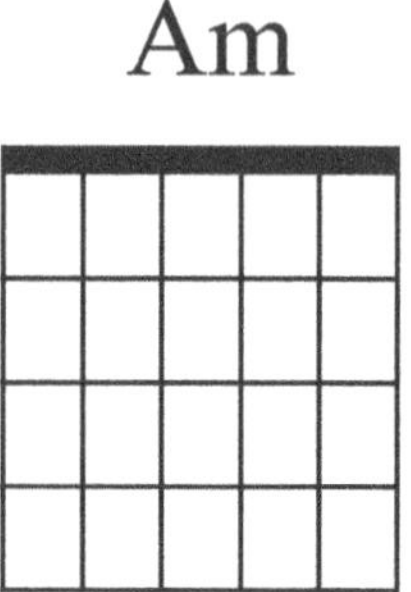

Use after page 34 of
Belwin's 21st Century Guitar Method 1.

Rock Boogie Chords: A5, A6, D5, and D6

1. Notate, on the tablature, the chords indicated in the treble staff.
2. Name the chords.

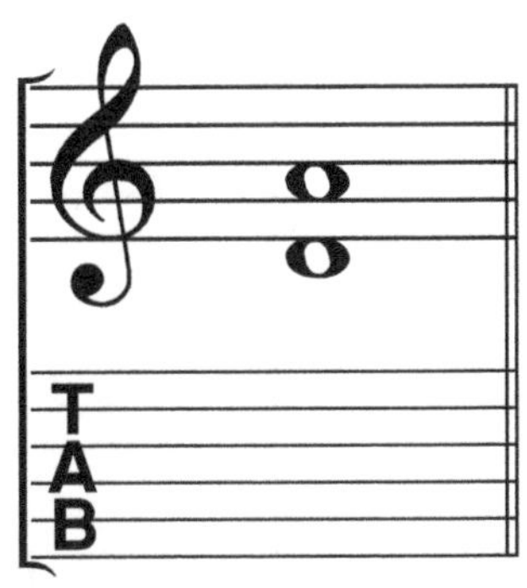

Fill in the chord frame diagrams to illustrate how the chords are fingered on the guitar fretboard:

A5

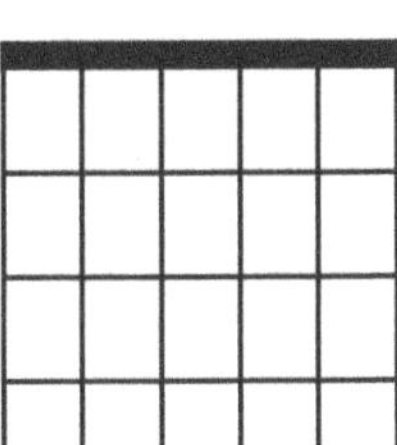

A6

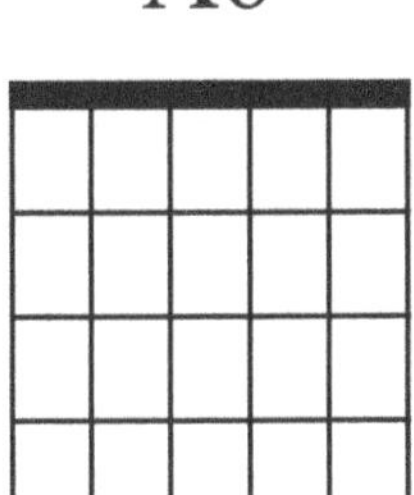

D5

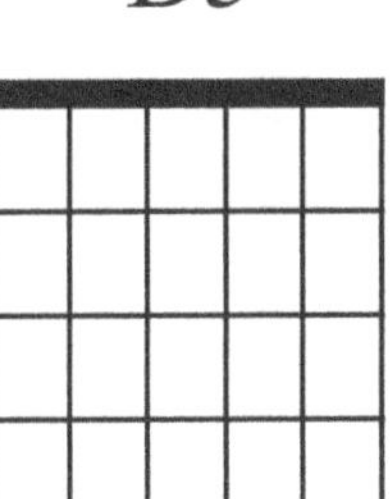

D6

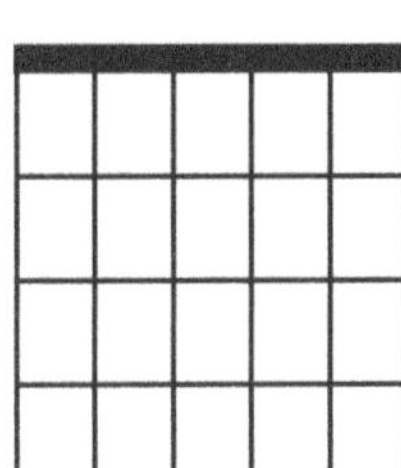

The chords A5, A6, D5, and D6 are illustrated in the following chord frame diagrams. Draw the indicated notes on the music staff:

D5

D6

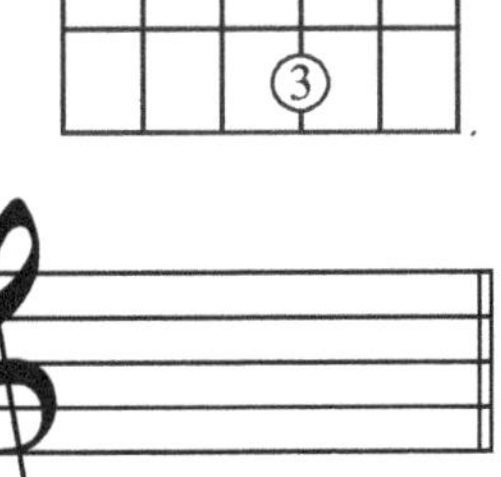

A5

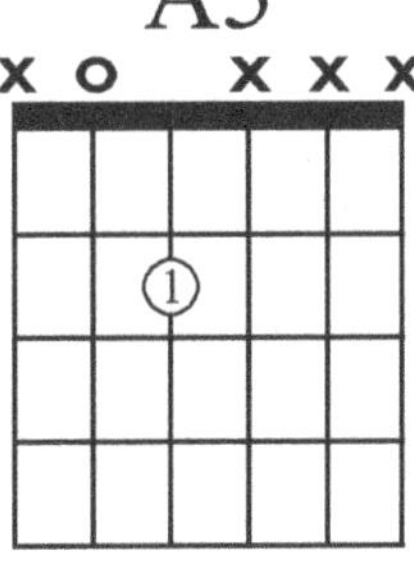

A6

Use after page 35 of
Belwin's 21st Century Guitar Method 1.

1st and 2nd Endings

The repeat sign tells you to go back to the beginning. On the repeat, skip the 1st ending and play the 2nd ending.

Here is a famous piece of music by J. S. Bach.

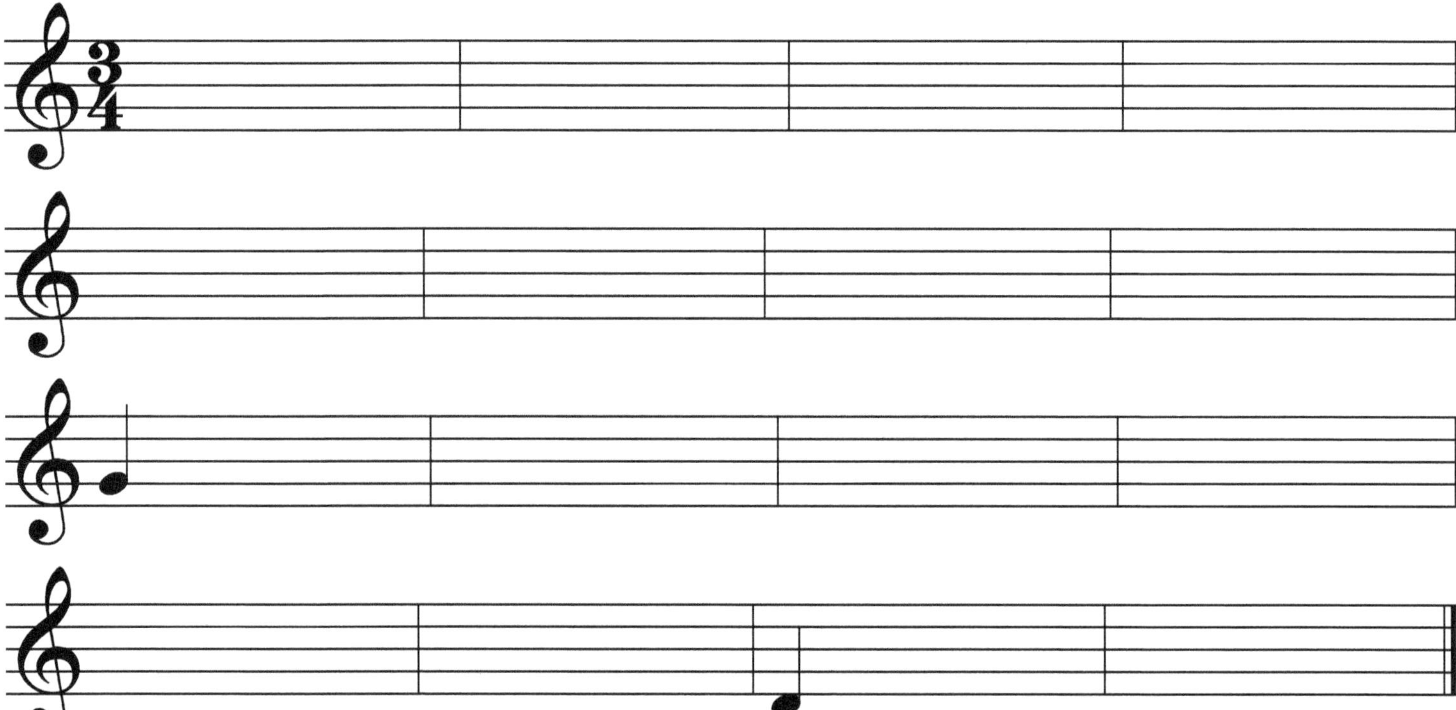

Write the piece of music from above as it would appear without the 1st and 2nd endings:

Now go back and play the song.

Chord Review

Name the notes and notate them in the tablature:

Name the notes and play them.

The Notes on the 6th String

Name the notes below:

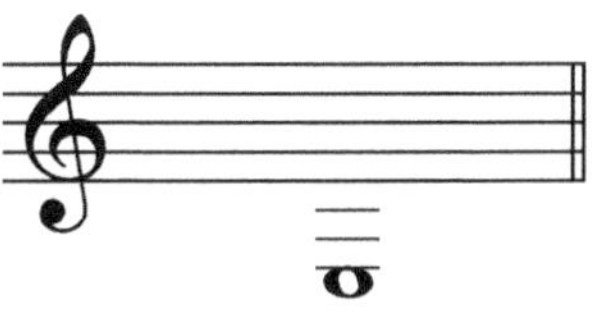  

This fretboard diagram indicates a note played with the ___ finger at the ___ fret of the ___ string. Its note name is ___ . Play the note and say its name.

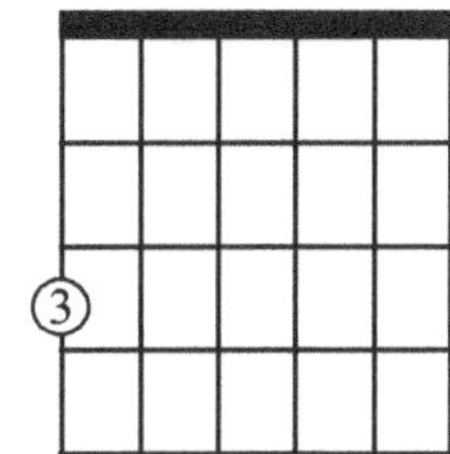

This tablature indication shows that the ___ string is to be played at the ___ fret. It will sound the note ___ . Play the note and say its name.

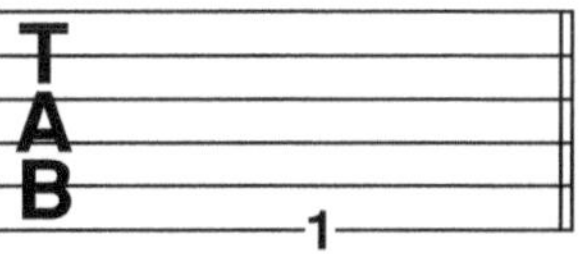

Name the notes indicated in the fretboard diagrams to the right:

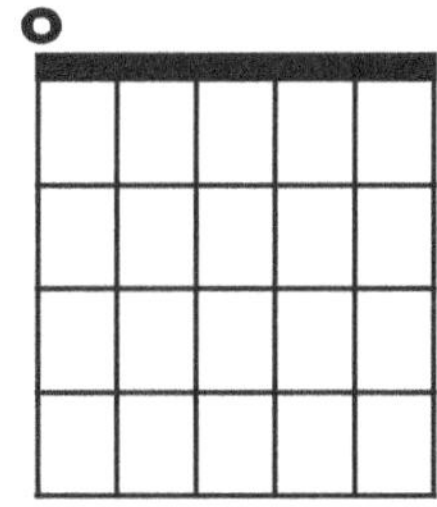 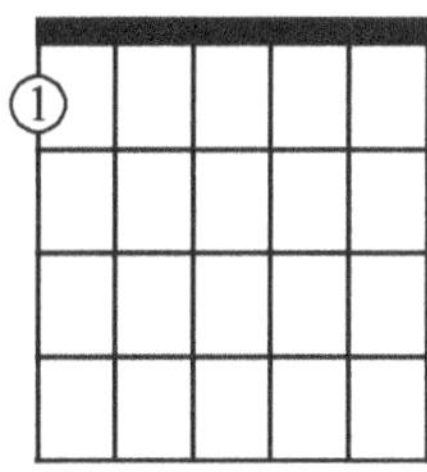

Draw the notes indicated in the tablature:

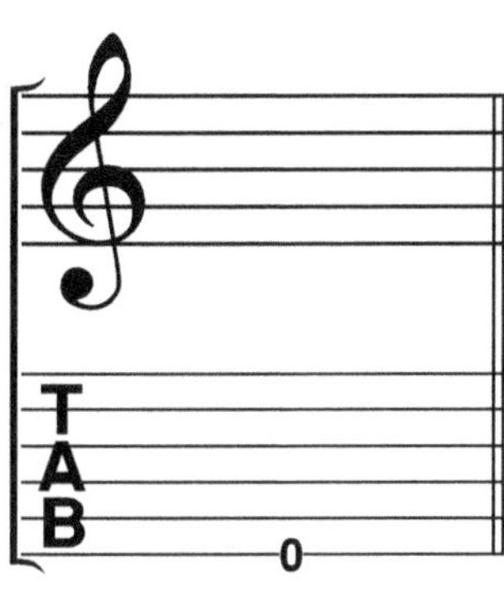  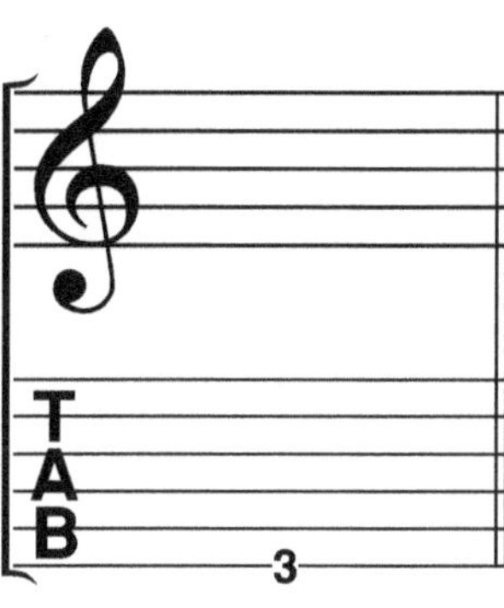

Name the notes and play them.

Use after page 38 of
Belwin's 21st Century Guitar Method 1.

New Riff Blues

"New Riff Blues" is based on a single-string riff (A Riff). It is then transposed to the 4th string (D Riff) and the 6th string (E Riff).

1. Draw the missing numbers in the tablature.
2. Play the song.

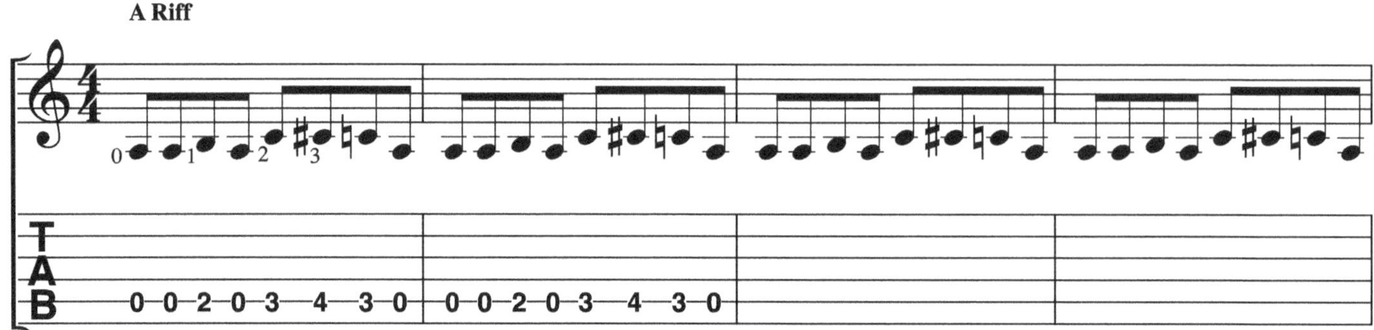

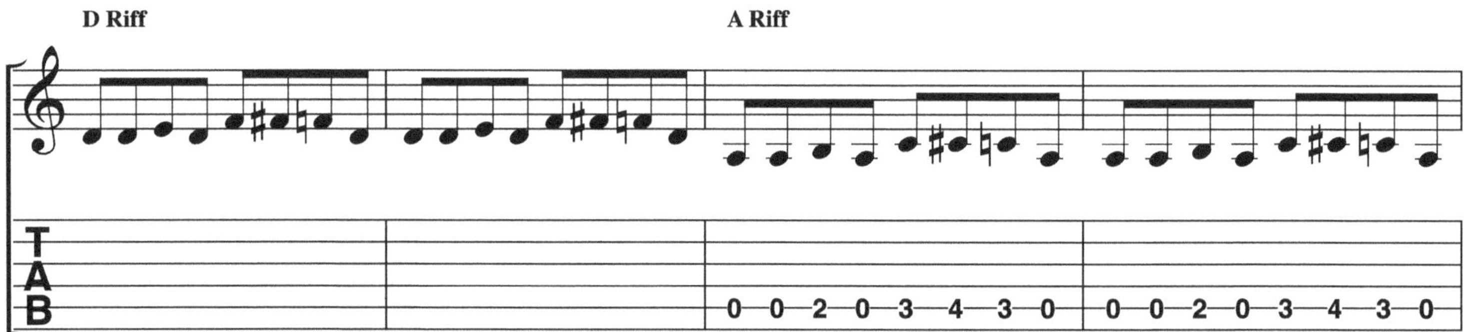

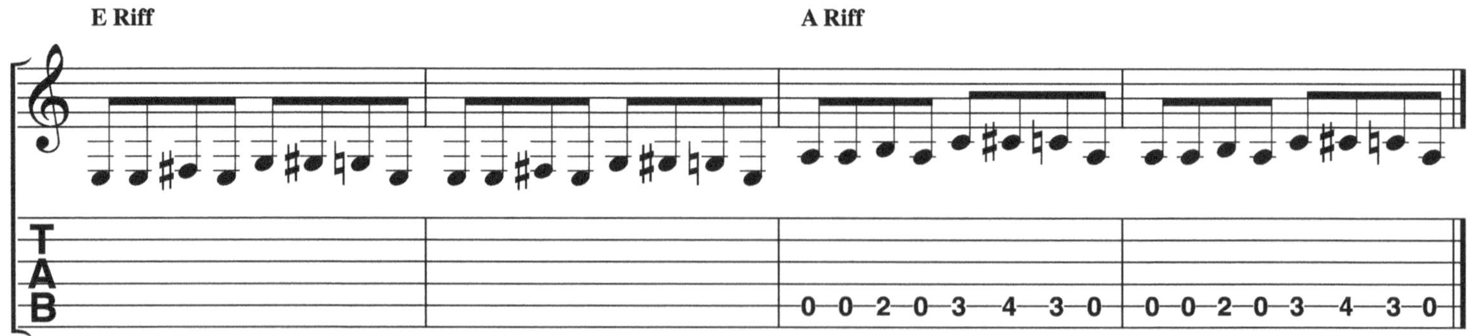

Use after page 39 of
Belwin's 21st Century Guitar Method 1.

More New Blues

"More New Blues" is a variation of the patterns played on page 39 of *Belwin's 21st Century Guitar Method 1.* This is a lead guitar solo that features one basic riff, an intro, and an ending. Fill in the missing TAB and music notation throughout. Also, fill in any missing slurs and hammer-on indications. Finally, play the song.

1. Draw the missing numbers in the tablature.
2. Play the song.

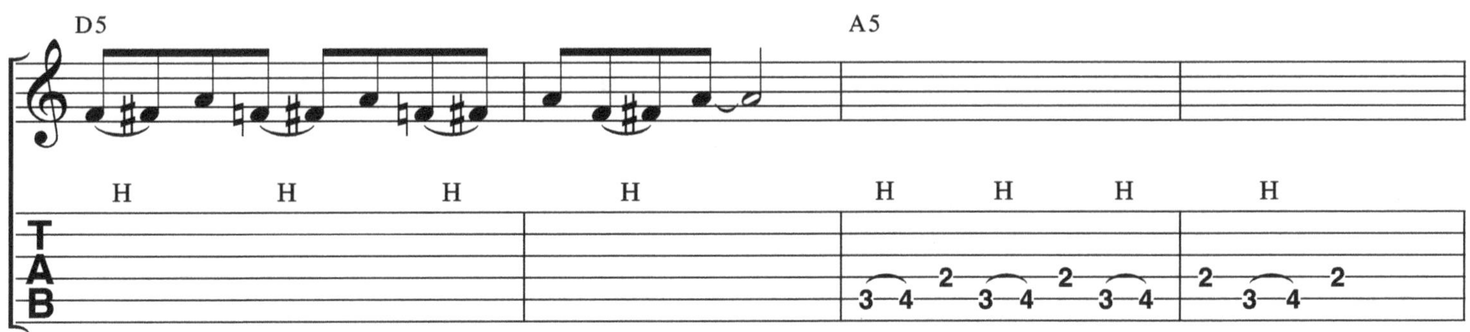

Use after page 40 of
Belwin's 21st Century Guitar Method 1.

The Full G, G7, and E Minor Chords

The full G, G7, and E Minor (Em) chords are illustrated on the chord frame diagrams.
Draw the indicated notes on the music staff:

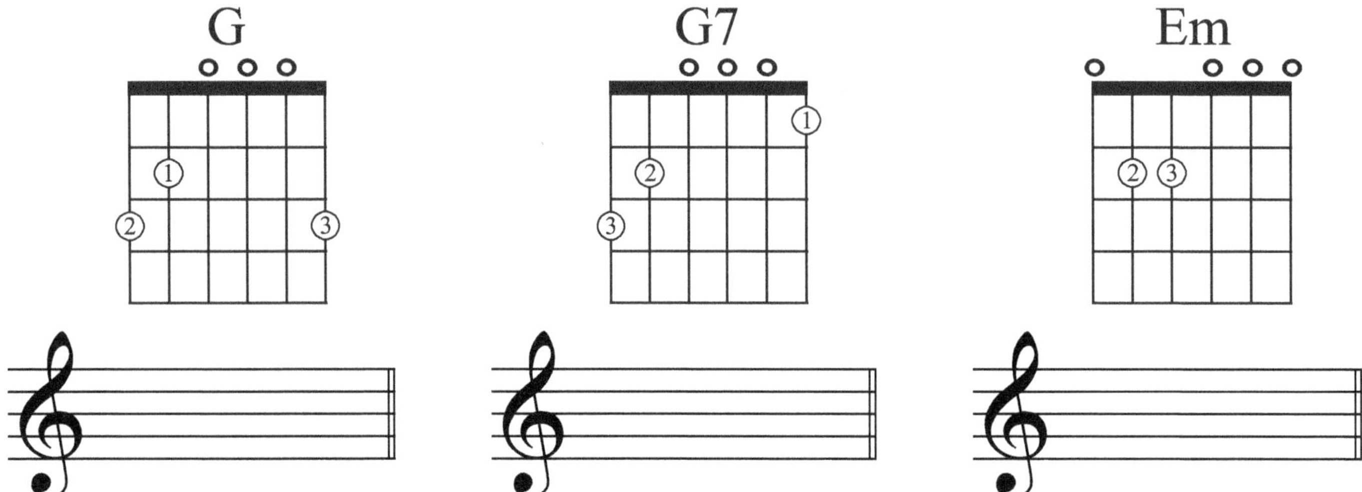

1. Notate, on the tablature, the chords indicated in the treble staff.
2. Name the chords.

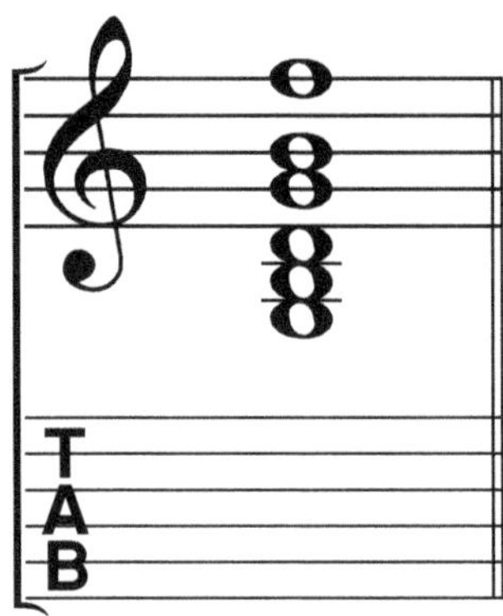
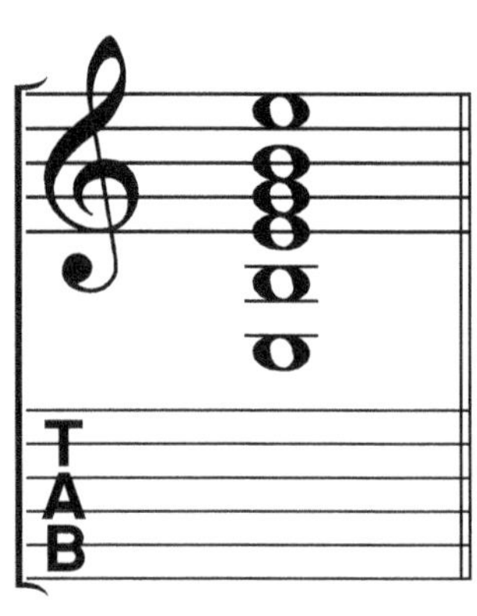
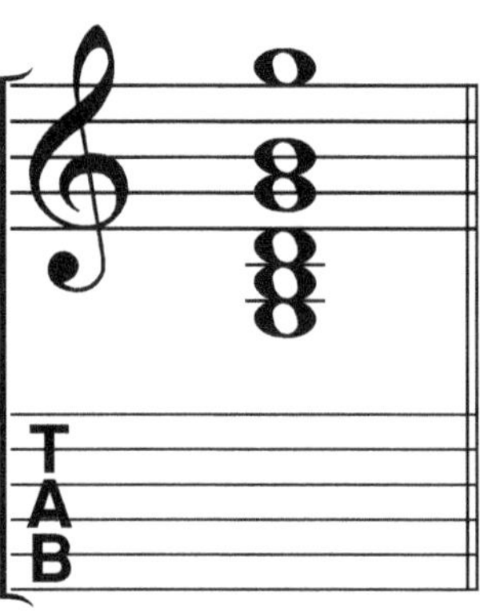

____   ____   ____

Fill in the chord frame diagrams to illustrate how the chords are fingered on the
guitar fretboard:

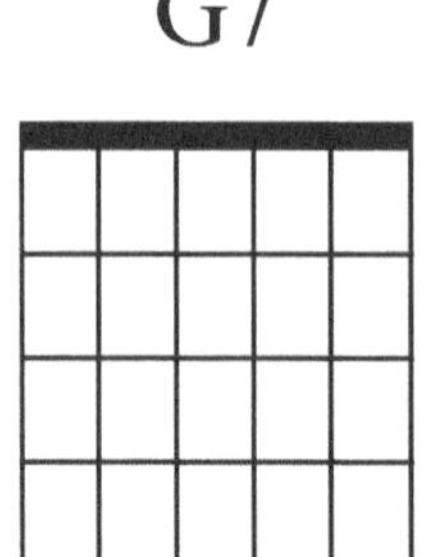

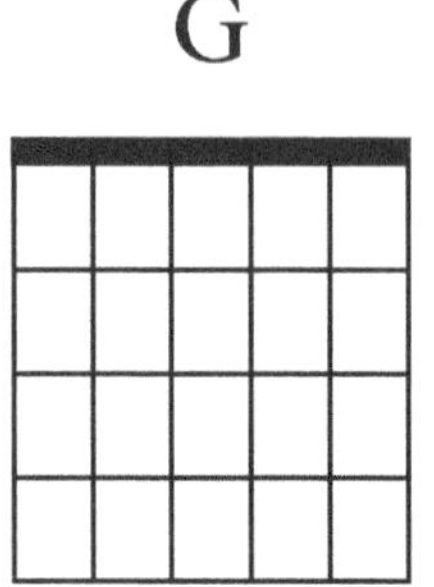

F♯ on the 6th String

Fill in the name of the indicated note:

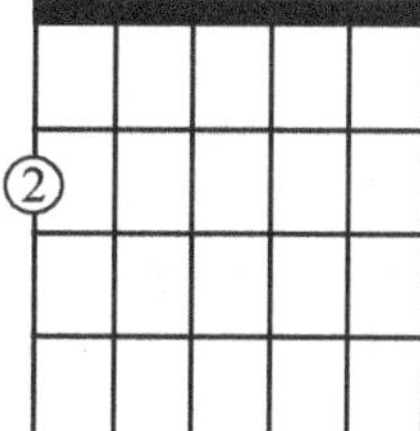

This fretboard diagram indicates a note played with the ___ finger at the ___ fret of the ___ string. Its note name is ___ . Play the note and say its name.

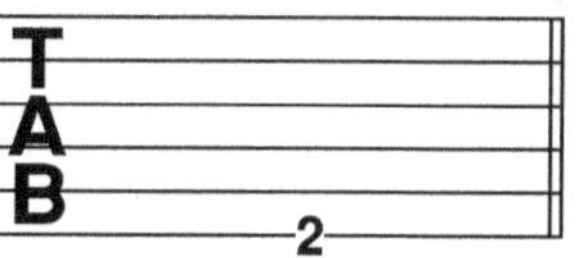

This tablature indication shows that the ___ string is to be played at the ___ fret. It will sound the note ___ . Play the note and say its name.

Note Review

Name the notes below, then play them:

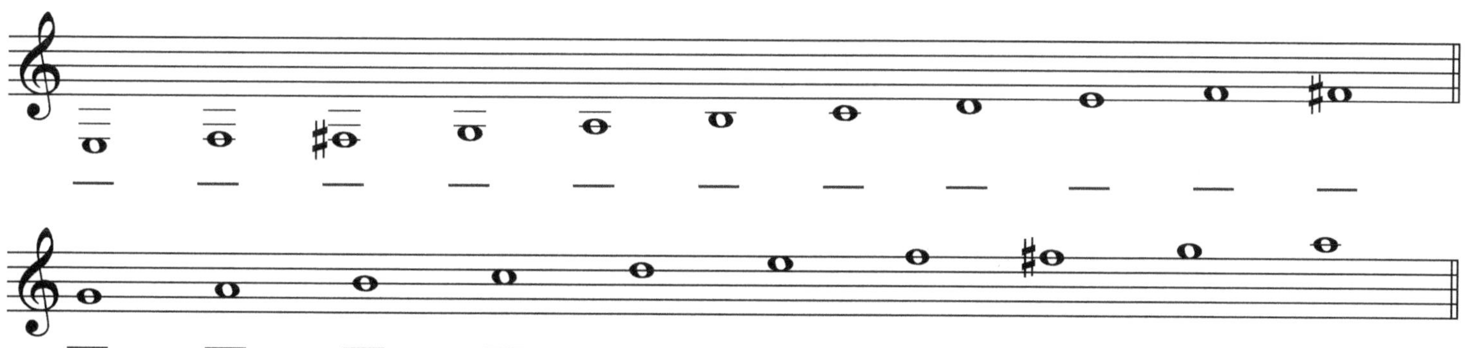

Rhythm Review

Add bar lines to the example below, then clap the rhythm:

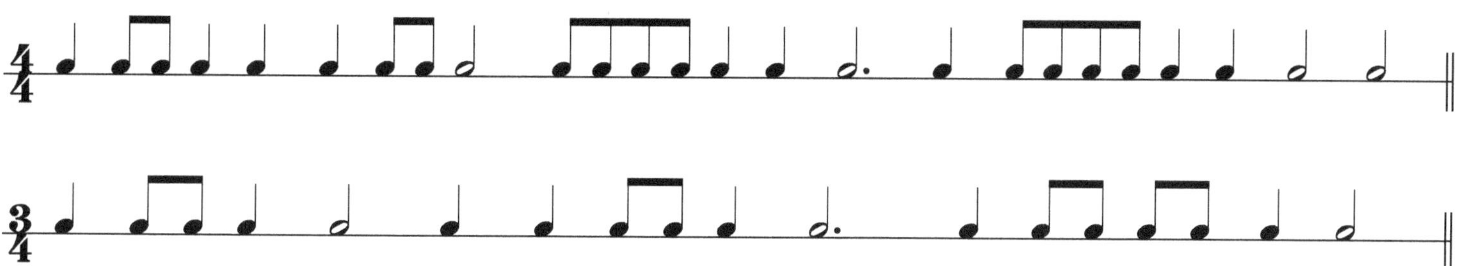

Use after page 41 of
Belwin's 21st Century Guitar Method 1.

AABA Song Form

"Power On" is a song written in AABA form based on the three power chords
we know. In AABA form there are two sections, A and B. The first A is repeated,
followed by B, and then we return to A. Fill in the chord frame diagrams to
illustrate how the chords are fingered on the guitar fretboard. Then, follow the
rhythm slashes and play "Power On."

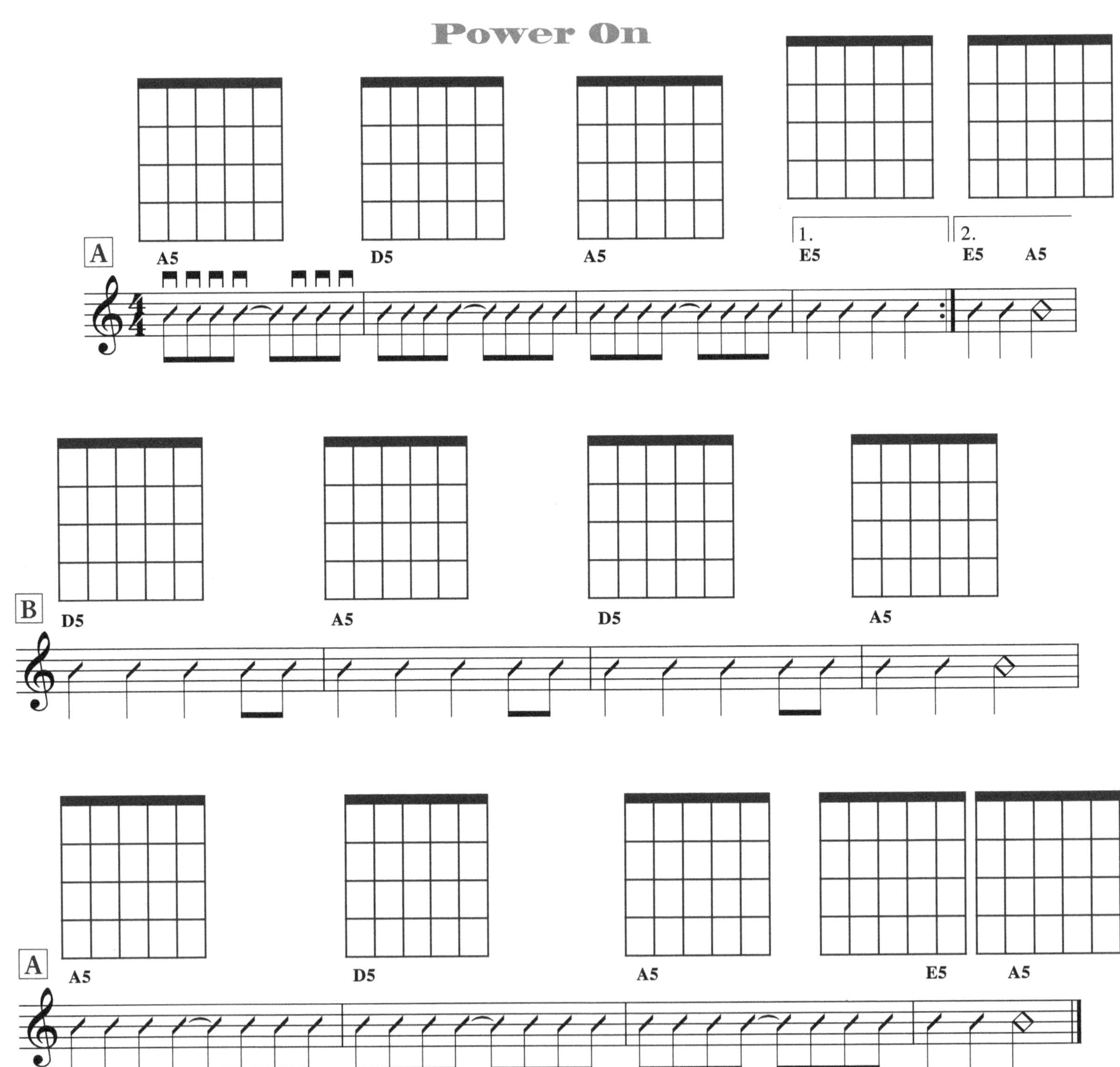

Chord Progression Review

Use after page 42 of
Belwin's 21st Century Guitar Method 1.

The chord progression G–Em–Am–D7–G is used in many songs. Fill in the chord frame diagrams below to illustrate how the chords are fingered on the guitar fretboard. Then, follow the rhythm slashes and play "My Heart's Got Soul."

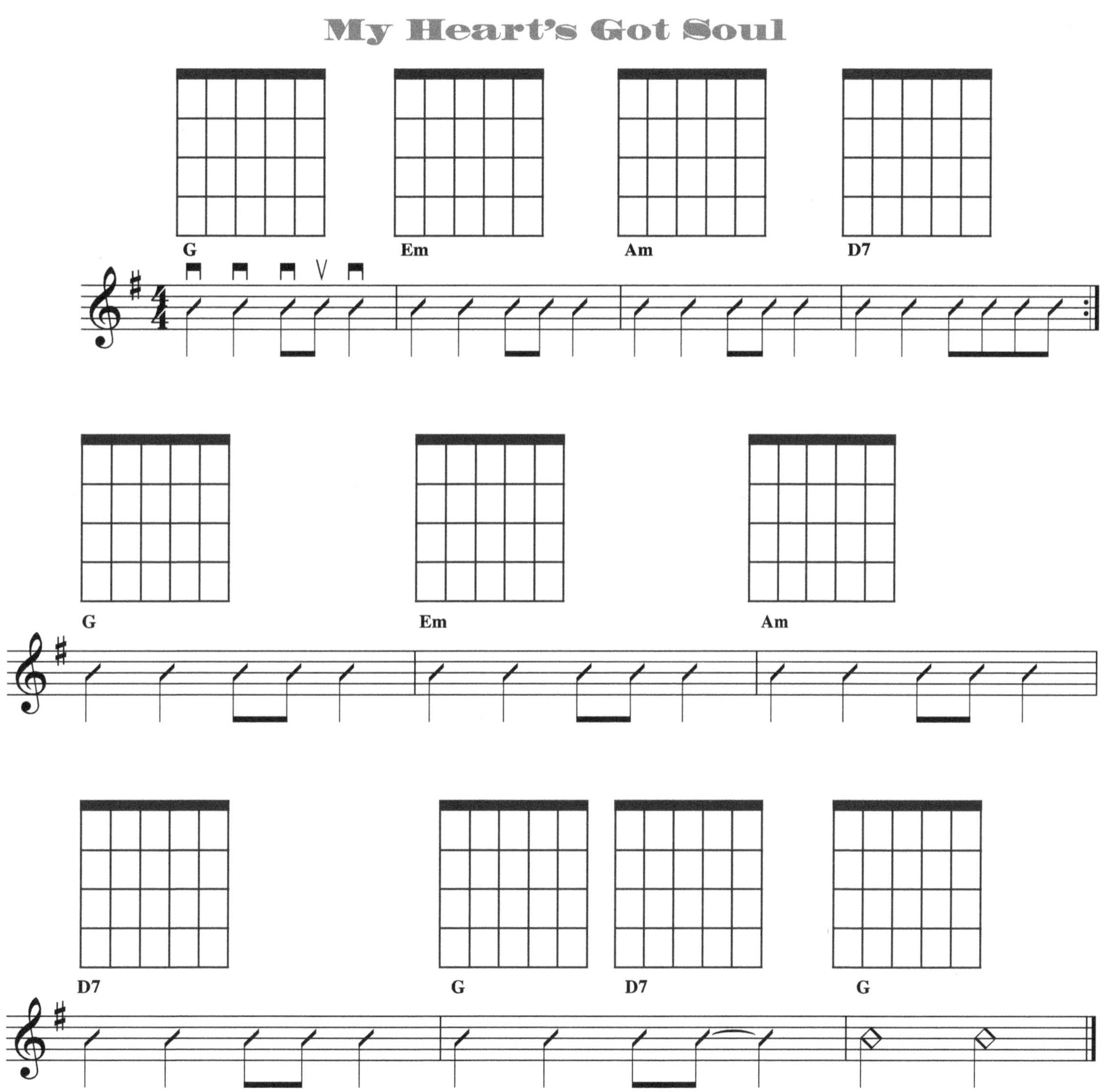

Use after page 43 of
Belwin's 21st Century Guitar Method 1.

The Rest

The duration of musical silence is indicated by different types of rests.

In $\frac{4}{4}$ time, a whole rest receives four beats:

A half rest receives two beats:

A quarter rest receives one beat:

An eighth rest receives half of a beat:

In the next exercise, fill in the missing beats with rests. Use only one rest in each measure, then clap the rhythm.

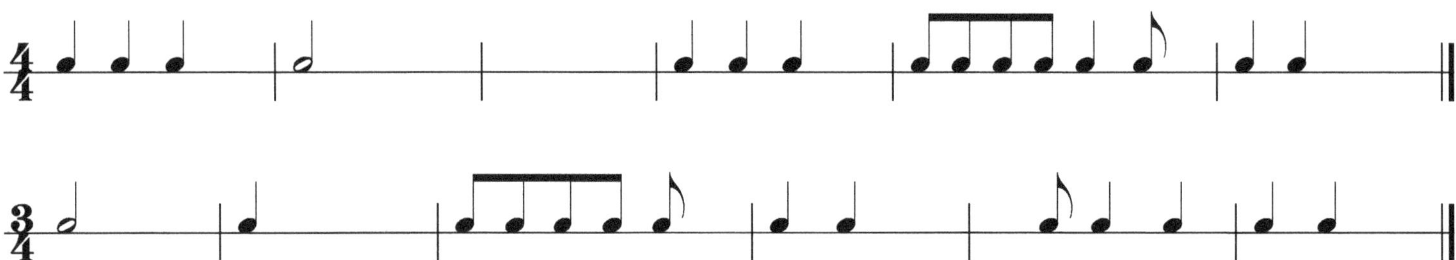

Add the bar lines, then clap the rhythm:

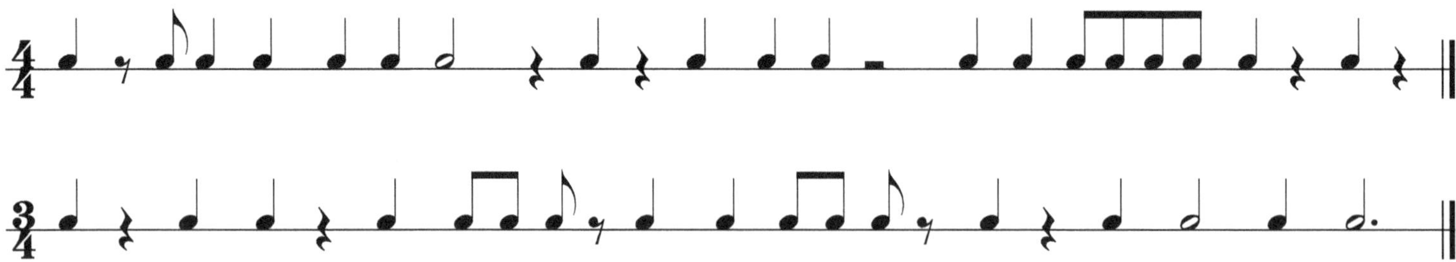

Fill in the blanks below:

One whole rest equals ___ beats.
One quarter rest equals ___ beat.
One half rest equals ___ beats.

Blues Composition

Below are four patterns you learned in *Belwin's 21st Century Guitar Method 1*: **1** is "Boogie Riff 2" (pg. 34), **2** is "A Riff" (pg. 38), **3** is "One-Grip Blues Pattern" (pg. 44), and **4** is "One-Grip Blues Lead Variation" (pg. 45). Each is shown in the key of A here, but you can transpose any of them to D or E. Write your own blues song below by assembling and transposing the patterns in a sequence that sounds good to you.

Blues Composition

Bonus Composition Exercises

In Rock Workshop 1 (page 28 of *Belwin's 21st Century Guitar Method 1*), we used an E chord shape in various locations on the neck to create interesting chord sounds. Here, you can create two new compositions using only the D chord shape.

D Chord Composition 1

1. Start on a D chord as indicated.
2. In measure 2, experiment until you find another location on the neck for the D chord shape that sounds good after the first D chord. Remember to let the open 4th string ring. Write in that fret number.
3. In measures 3 and 4, continue to experiment and find a series of chords using only the D chord shape. Fill in those fret numbers once you've found them.

Note: You can reuse any of the chords. You do not have to find a new chord for each measure. Your song can consist of two chords or more. Simply find a sequence that pleases you.

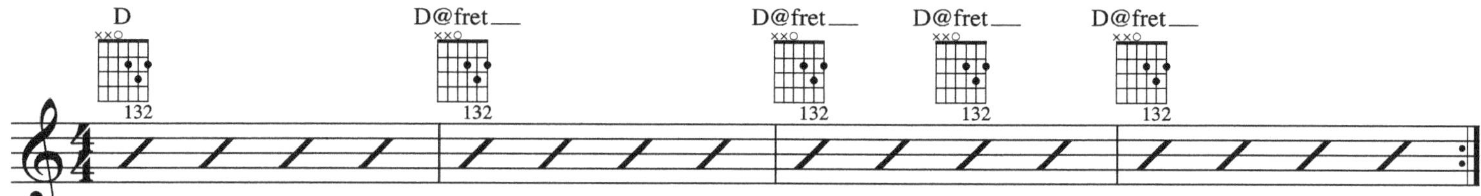

D Chord Composition 2

The following exercise is similar to the previous one, but your first two chords—D at the 7th fret and D at the 9th fret— will be provided here. After that, each chord is up to you.

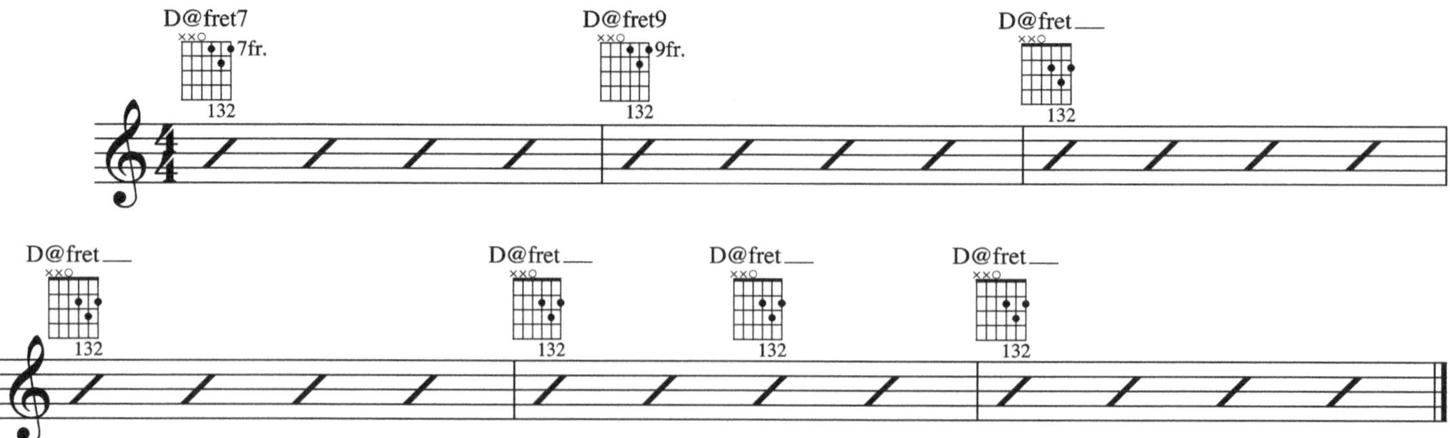

Guitar Chord Chart

Indicate the correct fingerings at the correct frets to complete this chord chart.

Am
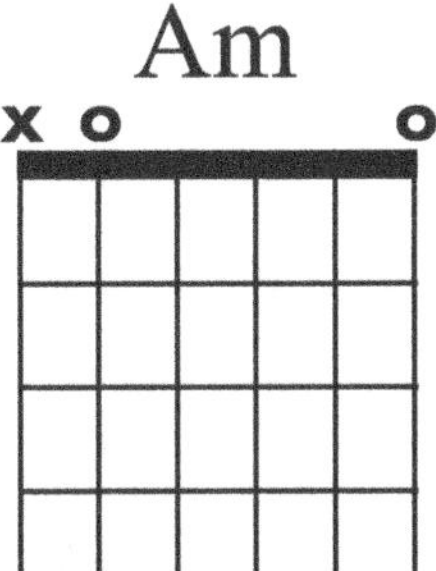

B7
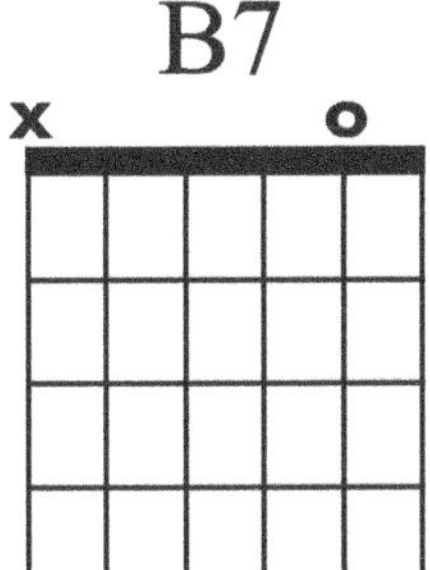

C
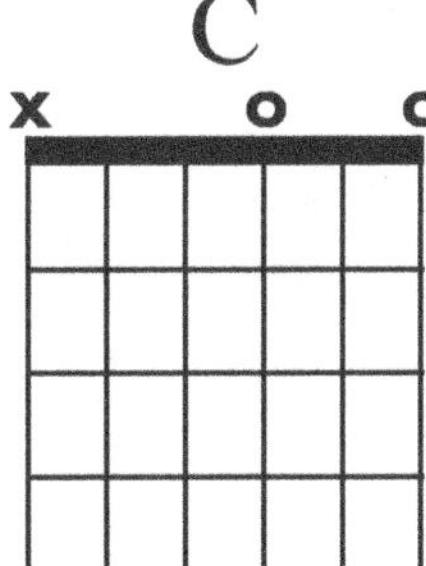

D
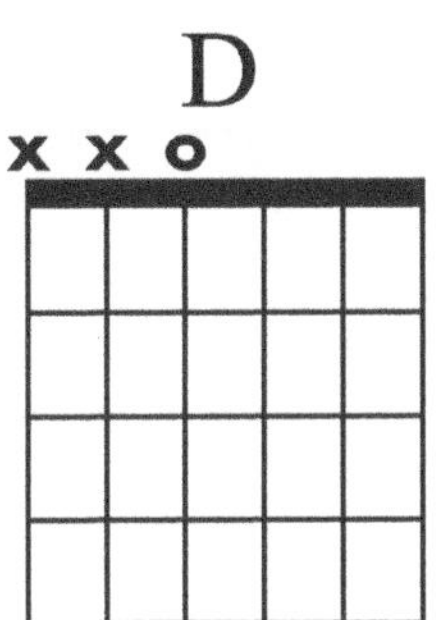

Dm
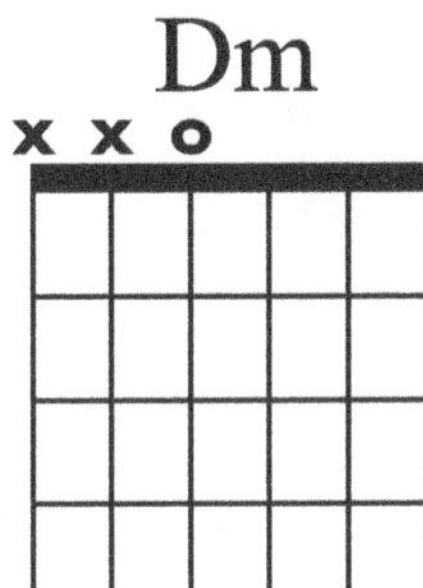

D7
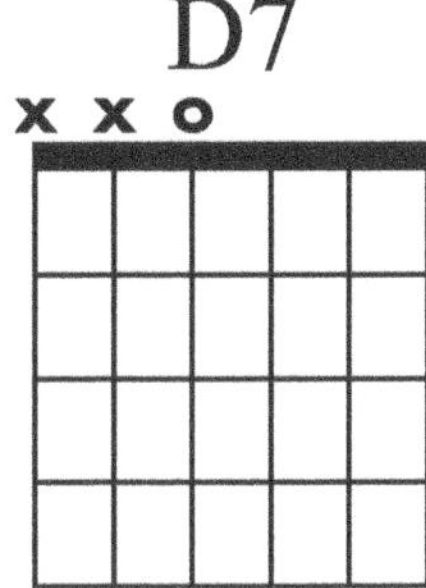

Em
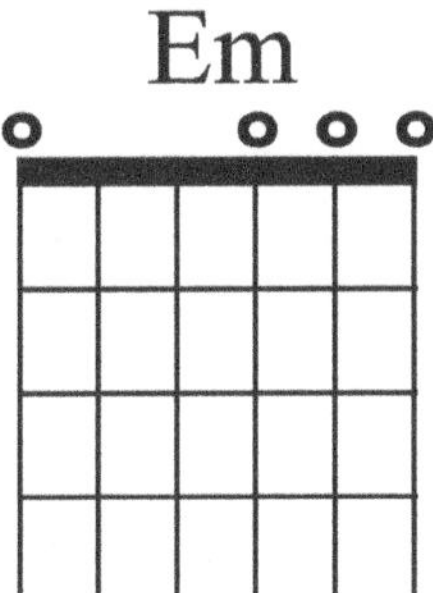

G
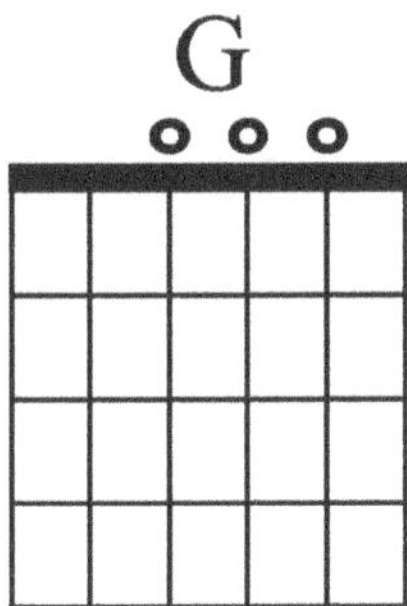

G7
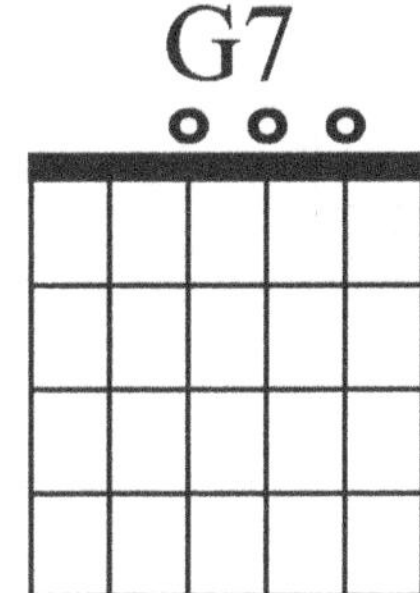

A5
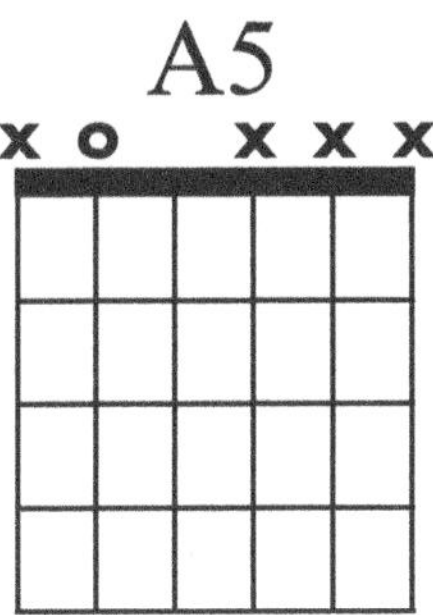

D5
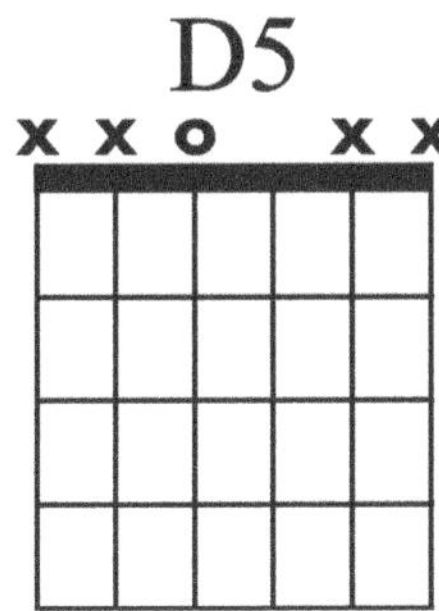

E5
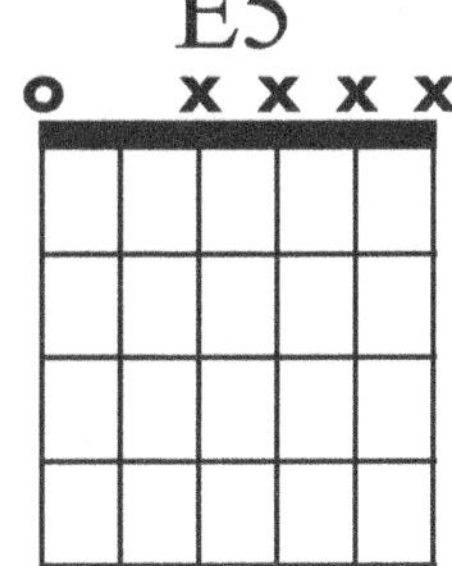

A6
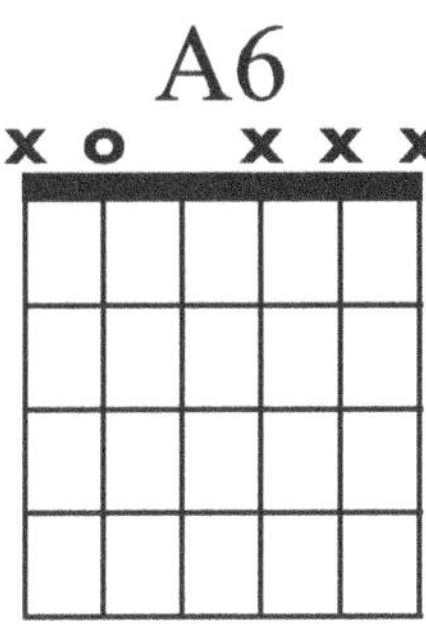

D6
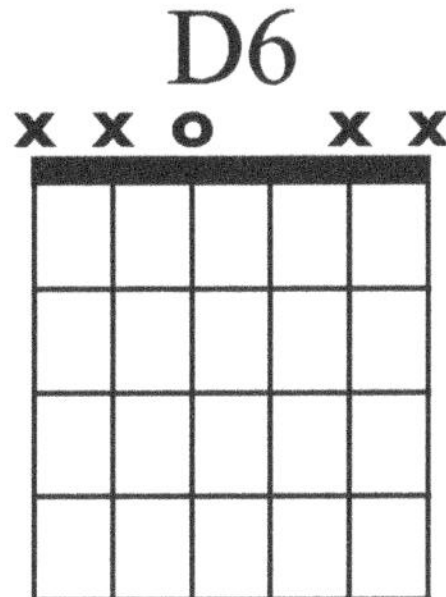

E6

Guitar Fingerboard Chart

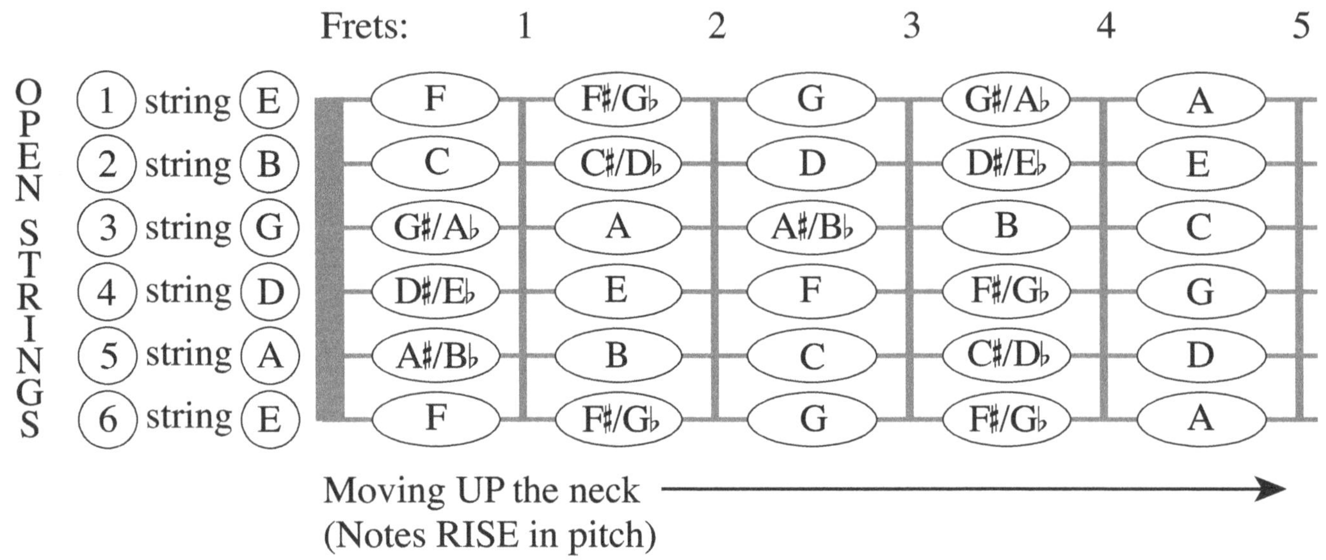